Best wishes to
The Onondaga County Public Library
SEP   2009
Readers.

Madhuri Sharma.
Sept' 09.

Through the Eyes of an Immigrant

Through the Eyes of an Immigrant

Madhuri Sharma

VANTAGE PRESS
New York

To my precious granddaughters

SHIBANI
MITALI
&
ILA

For being the light of my life and for completing
the circle of love.

Contents

Part III: Reflections

Acknowledgments

As I commence to list my appreciation of those who have made this book possible with their goodwill, input and suggestions, the first name that comes to mind is my husband, P. K. Sharma, for spending countless hours typing and re-typing the manuscript, for his insightful criticism and unflinching support every step of the way.

To Muriel Scott of Albany, New York, I am indebted for her valuable suggestions.

To Dr. Sakti Mookherjee of Syracuse, New York, my thanks for his erudition in narrating and translating the "mantras" chanted to the deity of Goddess Durga during the pooja festivities.

To Mr. B. S. Das of Davanagere, India, a "special thank-you" for his expertise on procedural practices of a Hindu wedding.

To Dr. Nithya Ramnath—thanks more than words can convey, for letting me write her story unedited.

A world of gratitude to my late parents for making me who I am. To Lord Venkateshwara, my eternal obeisance for His continued Grace and Guidance.

Thanks to Vantage Press of New York for working with me in publishing this book.

A special thank-you to Ms. Mumtaz Mustafa, Art Director of HarperCollins Publishers, New York, for designing the jacket cover.

Introduction

I embarked on writing my memoirs over two years ago, at my husband's encouragement. His faith and confidence were my inspiration and guiding force. With no formal training in creative writing or journalism, it was not easy for me to set out as a first-time writer, and more so in the golden years of my life. I wanted to draw my readers into a world of immigrants, through the eyes of an immigrant. As I traversed down memory lane, I realized that autobiographical writing could at times get to be intrusive and challenging, especially when candidly recalling one's own life experiences. In this genre, there is no access to fanciful flights of imagination as is possible in verse or fiction. It is an introspective journey that one has to undertake to know the feeling.

The first part of my book deals with our arrival on the shores of this fabled land over three decades ago, when my daughters and I followed my physician husband to the United States with our eyes and minds wide open. We encountered humorous, confusing and heart-warming adventures as we set out to embrace the culture of our new homeland. From getting a job here, learning which of my cultural ways to shed and which to keep, raising two girls in a society vastly different from the one I was raised in—it was a long road of continued education and adaptation.

The second part of the book focuses on our travels to

numerous countries which enabled us to widen our horizons, invigorate our psyche and enjoy the camaraderie of fellow travelers. Journalizing these experiences, saving photographs in chronological order, dipping into the "Discovery Series" given to us by the well-informed tour directors of each trip, and personal recollections helped me to put together this section in some detail.

In the third and last section titled "Reflections," I have dealt with the greatness of America as well as the currently ingrained weaknesses in the American system which, if not addressed in a timely fashion, have the potential of tarnishing the "American Dream."

Through the Eyes of an Immigrant

Part I

Transition

One

Moving to the U.S. from India

The prospect of our moving to America in the mid 1970s from the southern city of Chennai in India, started to take shape after months of personal contemplation and my husband's persistent desire to seek out newer pastures and a better life in distant lands—stemming in all likelihood from too much reading of Mark Twain's novels *Tom Sawyer* and *Huckleberry Finn* in his school days. "America" evoked in our minds a kaleidoscope of scenarios—the good, the scary, and the unknown. The human mind being credulous, thoughts of good times tended to prevail over all else. It was a land of opportunity, a "melting pot" of nations, and a country where poverty, squalor and hunger were virtually non-existent. The scary aspect was the permissiveness on moral fronts that was taking root within American culture. There was no knowing how deep it would get, or how it would affect our growing children. The unknown constituted almost everything else that we could not think of but would have to deal with, one day at a time.

I was a grown woman with an obligation to unfetter myself from the protective life I had known all these years in India. To my husband, it was as though the golden gates of opportunity in his chosen field were opening up, although a real fear of possible discrimination and rejection lurked in the back of his mind. Be that as it may, he was prepared to take the chances. Returning to life in India was always a viable option, in the event that things didn't work out here.

The U.S. at the time was welcoming foreign medical graduates to immigrate, and as a first step in that direction, he passed the qualifying examination offered at designated centers. Then started the protocol of interviews at the local U.S. Consulate followed by a series of medical examinations. A few days of anxious anticipation ensued and finally the long awaited day dawned that would decide our future. It was the final interview with the Consular Officer. In nervous excitement, I had chewed up my fingernails, forgot to take the pet poodle out for his morning walk, neglected to put the telephone back on the cradle, and missed unlocking the front iron gates until repeated clanging had me scurrying there to see the line up of the maid, the driver, and the gardener. My husband was as composed as he could possibly be. After a hurried breakfast, as he was ready to walk out of the door, I noticed that he had not knotted his tie and his socks didn't match.

At the U.S. Consulate, due process culminated in his receiving documents for an immigrant visa along with a humongous sealed brown envelope containing his chest X-rays which was to be hand carried and personally delivered to the immigration officer in the U.S. Excitement started to soar within me as the possibility of moving to the U.S.A. had now become a distinct probability. Older folks in the family advised us to keep things discreet and low key—partly to ward off the evil eye which proverbially denoted bad luck stemming from curses of undesirable people, and partly to remind us that in the aspirations and ambitions of mankind, there could always be a slip between the cup and the lip, meaning that things could still go wrong in spite of appearing to be all

4

set. To my two young daughters, it was all about journeying to a new country where all the "in things" in fashion and music originated, a country that housed Harvard and Yale, a land that the world looked up to.

The day arrived when my husband said his goodbyes and boarded the flight to New York. Seven U.S. dollars was all he was allowed to carry in foreign exchange. Friends in the U.S. helped out until he found himself a residency position in a premier teaching hospital in the Northeast. Within months, sponsorship papers for our daughters and me were filed and now it was our turn to make those trips for passports and visas.

As the news circulated among family and friends even at a low-key level, we were inundated with gifts and packages to be delivered to destinations in the U.S. In addition people offered advice based on what they had read or probably heard from the friend of a friend of a friend. "Guard your husband from the blonde women there," a witty acquaintance remarked.

"Don't forget your less-fortunate relatives back home," a well-meaning elder commented.

"Always be a cultural ambassador of India's ethnic heritage," our family lawyer advised. As our flight formalities were being confirmed, I felt increasingly deluged with mixed emotions—forsaking a comfortable life in the land of my birth for new beginnings in a country of promised prosperity. Further, the thought of leaving behind my widowed mother was heart-wrenching, although adequate arrangements were made for her stay and care. My innermost hope and prayer was that some day she would be able to join us in America.

As the day of our departure neared, the heaviness in my heart seemed to settle with a new gravity all its own.

The eve marked a traditional visit to the temple and the homes of elders for their blessings. The rest of the day was spent double-checking travel documents, tagging suitcases and ensuring they were within permissible limits, keeping sweaters handy in the carry-on baggage to counter the winter here, little knowing how low the temperatures could dip, and finally last minute reminders for rides to the airport. Prior to boarding, we stooped to touch my mother's feet in obeisance—a commonly practiced form of goodbye. With her trembling fingers on our heads, with tear-filled eyes and quivering lips, she simply said, "God be with you always." She knew, as well as I did, the ramifications of a move across the continents. Given her frail state of health, we might never see her again. The pace and pressures of life in America might also leave us little time to write to her frequently, or be at her side in times of need. However, we accepted what destiny had ordained for us.

The long ten-hour flight to London en route to New York was rumination time for me, while the girls enjoyed the in-flight movies, patronized the food carts, and intermittently fell asleep. Memories played themselves out like scenes off a float in a parade. Leaving behind a world that had seen childhood advance to womanhood, happiness and betrayal alternate with hope and despair, I was now headed to a new country, a new domain, a new culture and new demands on my adaptability.

After a brief layover at London, we were back to flying the friendly skies. Seven more hours to New York, the flight commander announced. Time to catch some sleep between the movies and the food carts. A pretty clear, crisp wake-up call informed us that we were due to land at New York shortly. It was the afternoon of Christmas Eve thirty-two years ago.

The Flight Commander announced over the PA system that we would soon be flying over Ellis Island and, with some luck, might be able to get a fleeting glance of the Statue Of Liberty, the edifice of a woman holding aloft a glowing torch. It was France's time-honored gift to America in 1884. Months later on a visit to Ellis Island, the erstwhile port of disembarkation to earlier immigrants, I had a chance to view firsthand the inspiring verse on the statue, composed by Emma Lazarus. The most meaningful lines of the inscription were:

From her beacon-hand glows worldwide welcome:
"Give me your tired, your poor,
Your huddled masses yearning to breathe free,
The wretched refuse of your teeming shore.
Send these, the homeless, tempest-tost to me,
I lift my lamp beside the golden door!"

Here lay the true meaning of welcome and freedom to all who chose to make America their home—the weary, the unwanted, the poor and the stifled—immigrants regardless of race, color or creed.

As we looked down from the aircraft, we set eyes for the first time on the skyline of New York City and its shimmering, snow-capped, towering buildings festively lit up in the spirit of the holidays. There were myriads of sparkling lights all around in varying shapes and sizes, beckoning visitors to this great land, with a welcome that no picture postcard could capture. My heart, my hopes, and my ambitions soared to hitherto unknown heights—we were indeed going to set foot on this coveted land of opportunity. The skyscrapers denoted columns of hope to an honest aspirant, while the many-hued glowing lights seemed like countless opportunities to the millions who had made it home here. I was jolted back to reality with the soft music playing in the background—Que Sera Sera, whatever will be, will be.

With that, the process of disembarkation began—through the walkway tunnel on to a hall of immense proportions, dominated by a sea of human faces. People seemed to be sprinting along their hurried paths to assigned destinations. Constant overhead announcements on baggage claim, customs and immigration, were routine jargon to the seasoned travelers, while my daughters and I were trying to catch up with the American parlance and accent. We managed to find our way through the long labyrinth of immigration lines to be eventually acknowledged as legal residents here with green cards. I felt as though we were being awarded a medal of honor for undertaking the exhausting eighteen-hour flight to the United States of America. A porter helped us with our baggage, which consisted of six large suitcases. We had packed everything in there—from Indian outfits to good-luck charms, elegant bedspreads to satin cushions, idols of family deities, coconut graters to cast-iron griddles, and sealed bags of Indian spices to tide us over the first few months. The customs officers let us through without much ado, probably because our baggage and the looks on our faces conveyed loud and clear that we were stepping onto Yankee soil for the first time. A few more paces ahead, my husband would be waiting to receive us, and the thought descended on me like a mantle of relief. As we parted ways with the porter, I gave him a five-dollar bill in appreciation of his services, feeling personally satisfied that it was a generous tip. He gave me a cynical look, handed the money back to me, saying, "You can keep it," and walked away. My initial reaction to this gesture was that even porters in this country could rise to such levels of magnanimity. My bubble was burst when I later learned that a measly tip of five dollars was, in all likelihood, an insult to him. We continued our trek towards the visitors' hall. It seemed like walking out of hazy trails into a large clearing where the sunshine was out to greet us. I soon spotted my husband in the milling crowds of visitors and in hours, we were on our way to Syracuse in Upstate New York, which would be home to us for the next three decades.

Our apartment looked bare and sparse. It was in stark contrast to our spacious bungalow in India in an upscale neighborhood. Furniture here consisted of sofas by day which converted to beds by night, a small dinette set in a corner of the living room which served as the dining, entertaining and study area, and a rickety floor lamp whose switch fell apart with the slightest vibration in the room. The functional part of it was the shade, brown with age, but still sitting in place. The beige and burgundy plaid sofa against the bare living room wall seemed to be less of an embarrassment, but not for long—its springs must have been in disuse for over a decade and any attempt to sit on it was tantamount to squatting on the floor. Across from it was a long rectangular object, carelessly covered with a tablecloth and meant to serve as a coffee table. A closer look at the contraption would reveal a well-taped cardboard box. The only saving grace in the room was a fairly new TV set, and the girls lost no time recognizing the fact. Popcorn, soda and kids' shows kept them occupied. The custom-designed furniture in India, the frosted glass windows overlooking the rose garden, the poinsettia pots adorning the mosaic entrance, and the neatly laid out brick walkway lined with day lilies, were all memories now. I made frequent trips to the bathroom to compose myself. *Was this the semblance of prosperity that we had envisioned?* I asked myself. My tears and emotions were sprinting way ahead of my reasoning capabilities. But I could not afford indulgences anymore. With a meager intern's salary of $800 per month in those days, this is all we could afford. Harsh realities had to be accepted, in the hope that better days were ahead.

Two

Adapting to Life in America

Exploring and adapting to life in a new country, and reaching out to new people, do stir up dormant qualities that transcend all ethnic and cultural barriers. I was determined to see the human differences as enriching rather than intimidating.

Given the hierarchy of moderate flexibility, I figured that adjustments should not be an insurmountable barrier, though the prospect of instant adaptability was never in the cards. A chauffeur, a gardener, a cook and a maid were the norms of an upper middle class home in India. This was possible due to the insignificant cost of labor in those days. I was very aware though, that once in the U.S., I had to quickly learn to be all of the above rolled into one and the earlier the better. I did realize that acquiring an enduring level of comfort in a new country wasn't going to happen overnight. My fluency in the English language, however, served as my initial window of communication with the many kind and caring people who lived in our high-rise building. Our two-bedroom apartment on the fourteenth floor seemed tucked away from human view. But that did not deter neighbors from leaving pastries, flowers, and candles at our doorstep to make us feel welcome. These unexpected gestures were more than uplifting for my already sagging morale.

Our first day in America was fairly uneventful. Suitcases were unpacked, spices and griddles found their

11

places in the kitchen cabinets, familiarity with stoves and dish washers established, and topography of the apartment building figured out. The children's admissions to the local convent school were in place, pending the entrance examinations in the New Year. I called India to inform my mother of our safe arrival—she had so many questions about the food, the weather, the children's schooling, and the neighborhood, but thankfully nothing about the apartment. She must have assumed we were living in some luxury penthouse. Our adventures began a couple of days later. My husband was on a twenty-four-hour rotation at the hospital and told me to call him only in a "dire emergency." As I set to prepare lunch for the day, I realized we had only canned products but there were no can openers in sight. My thoughts momentarily raced to the ease of life in India where vendors came with fresh vegetables and seafood to the doorstep each morning. Back to real life here, I debated whether the absence of a can opener translated to "dire emergency." I did not have access to a car nor did I know my way around. After half an hour of pondering, I was on the phone with the circulating nurse in the operating room. "What is the message for the doctor?" she asked.

"I need to know where the can opener is," I said.

She came back shortly thereafter and said, "There probably isn't one. Manage with what you have." Sure thing! I waited in the lobby downstairs looking for help. Within minutes, a kind older couple walked through the door and unhesitatingly solved my predicament by gifting me a can opener, which to this day I treasure as a souvenir. Over time, the Munsons became our "American parents" and never did a year go by without their presence at Thanksgiving dinner. They were there for us whenever we needed them; they guided us, advised us, and helped us blend mainstream into American culture. I did our weekly grocery shopping with them. But even grocery shopping in America has its challenges. Similar products had different names here. "Drumsticks" are common green vegetables in India, and favored in most delectable recipes. Not finding it in the produce section, I asked a store associate for help. Very graciously he escorted me to the meat department and pointing to trays of cut-up chicken legs, he said, "There you go. Fresh drumsticks just packaged." My hands-on learning process in the U.S. had already begun. Biscuits were called cookies, petrol was called gas, roadside pavements were referred to as sidewalks, and the list goes on.

Use of the washing machines was yet another experience. In India, maids did the laundry manually and got them pressed at street corners by ironing professionals. The first time at the washing machine, I was unsure of how much detergent to use, and emptied a whole bottle. Within minutes there were foamy suds pouring out of the machine. I rushed to the apartment office fearing I had broken the washer. A balding, pot-bellied gentleman addicted to chewing gum and with white froth lining his lips much like a camel on its regurgitated cud, escorted me to the laundry area, with a look that seemed to say, "How the heck did you manage to break a washing machine?" Disgusted with the looks and attitude of the man but steeped in concern over the machine, I silently walked alongside him. To my immense relief, the problem turned out to be "too much detergent." I was more than happy to part ways with the assigned help, vowing to frequent the laundry room only on weekends when he would be off duty.

The concept of buying "items on sale" was very alien to me. I was wary and suspicious of ads that said, "buy one, get one free"; or even better, "buy one and get two free." Why in Heaven's name would anybody give anything away for free unless there was something wrong with it? I guess I should have signed up for American Economics 101 to get a better understanding of this concept. The automatic car washes also seemed pretty intimidating initially but over time I learned that a lot of services in America are mechanized, cutting costs on time and labor. Today I patronize them all like no other.

An interesting incident comes to mind at this point, the details of which I recollect as though it happened yesterday. Three days after our arrival in the United States, I set out checking on bus routes, grocery stores and banks in the area. As I was waiting at the bus stop on this cold, dreary day, a friendly Caucasian lady walked towards me. She was tall and gaunt, dressed in a heavy winter coat, sporting leather gloves and matching leather boots. Her plaid Burberry scarf indicated a touch of class. She had a few wisps of curls that seemed to have strayed beyond the confines of her winter hat. I looked up at her with a smile. "Are you Indian?" she asked. Although I was dressed in Western clothes, it delighted me to meet someone who could place my ethnicity at first glance.

"Yes, I am," I replied, looking pleased.

"Which Nation do you belong to?" she continued.

A little perplexed, I replied, "The Indian Nation, of course."

With a faint smile on her lips and a brief coming together of her eyebrows, she said "What I mean is—which tribe do you belong to—where is your mother house?" I realized by now that we were not on the same wavelength. But the conversation continued anyway.

I told her "My mother house, father house, and uncle house are all in India." As for the word "tribe," I interpreted it to be "caste," forgiving her for not better expressing herself. "My husband is a Brahmin of the priestly class and I am a Kshatriya of the warrior class," I said. In the meantime, her bus pulled in and waving me goodbye with her gloved hand, she departed. I never ran into her again but I had, for sure, learned the difference between the two words—American Indian and Indian American. Subtle as it may seem, the in-depth nuances were far-reaching.

A week after our arrival in the U.S. was New Year's Eve. Partying, merrymaking, and ringing in the New Year at the stroke of midnight were the order of the day. Our hostess was a gracious American lady, past middle age with graying hair, blue eyes, and an inviting countenance that I can recall even to this day. The twinkle in her eyes and the unceasing smile on her lips as she greeted her guests, made her so unforgettable. Her perfectly tailored gray dress with matching shoes, spoke volumes for her high-end tastes. Shortly into the socializing, my eyes fell on her shapely legs which seemed unusually gray to me. I quickly shifted my gaze to her arms, which however looked normal for a Caucasian. My brains started working overtime to figure out the color discrepancy. My mother's parting words of advice came to me in a flash—"You are going to a new country," she said. "The first few months, be careful of what you touch, and what you eat—there could be so many contagious diseases out there." That was the "Eureka moment!" That was the answer I was seeking. In my mind, I concluded that this lady had to have a contagious skin condition on her leg, accounting for what I saw. Every time she came around with trays of pastries, cookies and other delicious eats, I would politely pass, making sure I didn't eat anything she had touched. My doctor husband, on the other hand, was heartily enjoying the treats with no inhibitions whatsoever. I told myself, "Obviously, he has no fear of catching the contagion." In my medley of confusion, a brief interlude of calm seemed to suggest that I take a closer look at her legs for any visual patches or disfigurement. But no, they seemed so evenly gray! Back in my own little world of suspicion, I told myself, "This is the age of medical marvels, and more so in the U.S. Things here can be fixed for cosmetic acceptability!" Hot tea or coffee was always okay, I remembered my mother saying, since germs didn't exist in that medium. I hastened to pour myself steaming hot coffee and circulated among the guests until the goodbyes were said. Once we got on the road, I wasted no time bringing up the contagion issue with this medico I was married to! He split his sides laughing like there was no tomorrow, and soon enough I learned about the pantyhose—a fashion accessory unfamiliar to most women in India.

With the advent of the New Year, our daughters were accepted to the all-girls convent school in town and they took to their surroundings like ducks take to water. The freezing January temperatures did not bother them nor did the new ambiance. Weeks rolled into months and life was beginning to fall in place. As a surgical resident, my husband had to work long hours in the hospital, necessitating the need for me to start driving. Two weeks after our arrival in the U.S., I had applied for a reciprocal driving license. To that end, I showed up at the Department of Motor Vehicles on the appointed day. It was determined that I did not need to take a road test (thankfully so) but I was required to pass a written test and a vision test. I had obtained an international driving permit from India, after clearing the driving test there. As normal as it sounds,

16

memories of that day in India will always remain a nightmare to me. The test area was cordoned off with orange drums in a large figure "8" formation. The candidate was required to drive forwards through the twists and turns in the cordoned area and then retrace the same path backwards, without knocking down a single drum. This called for more maneuvering skills than routine highway driving. The palpitations in my chest cavity probably became more audible than the sound of the car engine. My knees had turned jelly-like, but I desperately needed them both to pass the test. The examiner remarked, "How are you going to drive on highways in America, if you can't take this simple test?" I saw no sense at all in his comparison. With beads of perspiration on my forehead stemming from nervousness and a sweltering eighty-degree temperature around, I inwardly viewed this process as a trip to the slaughterhouse. I finally took the test rear-ending a few drums in the process. No major damage excepting dents to my ego. The inspector declared that I had barely passed the test but should retake it for better scores. I wasn't looking to become a Driving Instructor, and I certainly wasn't coming back either. I had aced the written test at the DMV here bearing in mind that people in the U.S. drove on the right side of the road as opposed to the left in India. The cars here were much larger than I was used to, and keeping to the right did not make driving any easier. In the winter the roads were invariably snow-covered and icy. A few fender-bender accidents, some slipping and sliding into the roadside ditches, and I was well on my way to becoming a fairly seasoned driver.

It was a bright beautiful morning, with the frosts and freezes of the past few days seemingly stepping aside to welcome the rare appearance of the sun in the clear skies. From the 14th floor apartment of our high-rise building, overlooking the incessant downtown traffic, the snow-ploughed roads looked like miles of black tapestry fringed with white. Robins and sparrows had not chosen to come out of hibernation, nor did the rooster announce the dawn of day. Nothing about this day would have warned me about the comedy of errors that was soon to occur.

With the children gone to school and my household chores done, I prepared to go to the hospital to pick up my husband who was getting off duty from his Emergency Room rotation. As always, I indulged in wearing a "sari" complete with a streak of red vermilion powder on the parting of my hair and a red dot on my forehead. These were traditional markers of a married Indian woman and I was still on "just off the boat" mode. As I walked into the Emergency Waiting Room, which at the time seemed nothing like a crowded railway station I had imagined it to be, a kindly looking older nurse came up to me and said they could take me in right away—it was one of those rare days when the place wasn't seething with patients. I introduced myself to her as a Resident's wife, but neglected to mention why I was there. She asked me if I had "signed in" and I replied, "Well, in fact I was looking for the Visitors' Book." Looking pretty amused, she seemed to be focusing on my forehead and beyond as she continued the conversation. "You do have a sense of humor," she said and then went on to ask me if I had my health insurance card. I assured her that I did possess one but not on me. She replied, "We'll do the formalities later," and let me in through large double doors, down a corridor where gurneys and wheelchairs were parked with patients hooked to intravenous infusions, past the nursing station where the doctors made notations on charts while sipping coffee. I thought the trek would never end, although silently appreciating the nurse for skipping the protocol in an attempt to help.

She seated me in a nearby cubicle, drew the curtains for privacy and promised to return shortly. *This must be where I was to wait until my husband was ready,* I thought. As I reflected over the past few minutes, I attributed all of this to the outstanding efficiency of American hospitals, their system of identification for patient security, the gracious demeanor of the nursing staff, and possibly the superb patient care that I was not there to avail. Sure enough, in a few minutes, the nurse was back, this time escorted by a tall middle-aged doctor in a long white coat and a calm, reassuring stance. I noticed that he also, for some reason, seemed to avidly focus on something beyond my forehead. He exuded an air of confidence, as he prepared to get to work. I was somewhat bemused, but respectful of these professionals and the protocol in an American hospital. So I quietly waited.

Looking back now, I am sure he might have had a few medico-legal questions that he held off on. While the nurse got the sterile instrument tray ready, the doctor came a step closer to better view my vermilion-laden parting on the head. It probably did look like dried-on, caked-on blood. But all he said to me was, "This needs to be cleaned up, a few sutures and you'll be on your way." My eyes widened. Numbed beyond belief, I staggered out of my chair, mumbling, "Nothing is wrong with me. I am only here to pick up my husband." The embarrassment that ensued had to be seen to be believed. At that juncture, my husband walked in, rendered the much-needed cultural explanation, and we were out of there, with me literally sprinting to the parking lot! While driving back home, I ranted and raved and vowed never to wait around an E.R. again. My husband simply said, "How could you be so stupid as to walk into an E. R. in America with a ton of vermilion on your head?" That was the last of my indulgences in those practices. I decided then and there to drop some of the outwardly visible cultural differences.

With the advent of a car at my disposal, I ventured out looking for a job to supplement the tight family income. Entry-level jobs in banks were easy to come by, I was told. At each of the banks known to be hiring, I filled applications in person and waited for an answer. Much to my chagrin and disappointment, I was summarily rejected on the grounds that I was overqualified. I could not fathom the hiring system here—wasn't being overqualified better than being underqualified? I asked myself. *Maybe it was my foreign-sounding name,* I thought. But in this land of opportunity where racial discrimination is frowned upon by law, that could not be it. Maybe it was my Asian looks. But they hadn't even interviewed me to conclude that I looked different. In India, the waiting area for prospective interviewees would be packed. Higher the qualifications, better the candidate's chances. Could it be that the employers here feared a high turnover hiring overqualified candidates? In my mind's eye, I scanned every section on those applications, but drew a blank. Undaunted, the next day I set out again, a trifle wiser this time. Under "educational qualifications" I listed only my high school diploma, and no further. My college degrees and positions on the teaching faculty were of no relevance now. I desperately needed a job. And bingo, within the hour I was interviewed and offered the position. The personnel manager however had a word of advice for me. "Young lady," he said, "if I were you, I would at some point, think of going to college and onto grad school. You have what it takes to get there." I merely smiled and nodded rather awkwardly. I had ultimately landed myself a job, and that was all that mattered at the time. Being an academician by training, this entry-level job of waiting on bank customers, doling out cash, and reconciling accounts at the end of the day seemed very frustrating. But the choice was not mine to make.

In the grand scheme of things, my husband completed his residency and became an attending physician. Life on a shoestring budget slowly gave way to affordability and a nicer home. Frequenting discount stores became a thing of the past, though my husband fondly recalls with pride his cherished days of "sidewalk and moonlight sales!"

Over the years, I adapted to Western culture reasonably well though a small part of me remained Indian. I was comfortable in pantsuits year round and patronized cotton tops and trousers in summer. My ethnic "sari" continued to be my outfit for dressy occasions. For the most part, I cooked Indian food at home and we ate out on birthdays and anniversaries. A typical home-cooked meal consisted of rice, lentil curry, a vegetable dish and yogurt. Chicken and fish were fixed primarily for our children or for invited guests. American friends were invariably very compliant and enjoyed Indian curried food, although I always had "lasagna" and "pizzas" as standbys.

American generosity and philanthropy have and to this day continue to evoke the greatest admiration in me. Their spirit of charitable giving, whether it is to support a church bake sale or orphaned children in a house fire, a blood donation drive, or a sponsored marathon walk, has been admirable. When humanitarian aid was needed in any country, the American relief agencies were in the forefront rendering assistance. Over the years, concern for human welfare had become a time-honored tradition in America.

When our children grew up to be teenagers, my own upbringing in India seemed to rekindle itself. But we were in a different country now, with different norms of life and expectations. I encouraged them to believe in themselves and their goals, while retaining the paramount importance of values and morals. There has always been an indomitable strength in the concept of balance. They were taught to regard our ethnic culture with unquestioned respect rather than curiosity. Dating was discouraged during school years because we strongly believed that there would be enough opportunities later in life for all of that. Our daughters were second-generation Indian Americans. Generational and cultural conflicts were going to surface and I considered it as part of the price we paid for migration. Acquiring American identity while retaining some ethnicity alongside was like paddling two canoes at the same time. And on choppy waters at that.

Time seemed to take on wings, and our older daughter entered high school, soon to be followed by her younger sister.

The prom in our older daughter's senior year was the most anticipated event in the school as it was in any American school. Unsure of what all of this entailed, I talked to our Western peers and fellow parents to discuss this significant social event. I gathered that the prom was a formal dance held at the end of the high school academic year. It symbolized the culmination of one phase in life and the beginning of the next, giving the teenagers a new perspective of freedom and independence. Much to my chagrin, I was told that a predetermined guy from the boys' school in a tuxedo and a limousine would, with our permission, escort our daughter to the prom. The party would end in the wee hours of the morning when the prom seniors would return to their respective homes. The very prospect sent a chill down my spine. Who would be this predetermined guy and when was he going to come out of the woodwork? High school years were the phase when kids had hormones racing up and down their systems. How was I sure our daughter would be safe? A zillion possibilities crossed my mind. This could be walking a razor-thin edge of promiscuity. I had forbidden dating in high school, and I certainly wasn't going to allow it now in the form of a social event. Be that as it may, I was determined to enforce the median line of ethnic acceptability.

Our daughters heard me out in pristine silence. The resigned look on their faces reflected the foregone conclusion in their minds. There were no protests or rebellion from them. The power of the unspoken word was never before so effective. My husband and I discussed it for days. He tended to relent some while I continued to stand my ground. The only possible compromise was—we would escort our daughter to the prom, wait around for as long as it took and bring her back home. To our daughters, such a thought was the peak of embarrassment and they categorically told us that they much rather skip the event than be seen escorted by parents. And that was the peaceful closure to what might otherwise have been a controversial issue.

I hoped that we could persuade them to attend the prestigious university in our very own hometown, in spite of the prevalent mode of children aspiring to move to distant universities away from home. I mentally worked overtime to accomplish this as innocuously as possible. I decided to simultaneously look for a job in the university. This I did without much ado and before long I found myself in training, dealing with student accounts and related budgetary adjustment processes. A pretty involved learning process it turned out to be, familiarizing myself with the nuances of such issues as student accounts, financial aid, and college work-study. The following year I was asked to prepare to be a commissioned notary public, as part of the job requirements. Compliance came easy to me by now, and this was no exception.

It was mid June and the long awaited high school graduation had arrived. Anticipation and excitement filled the air—our daughter looked absolutely radiant in her white gown with a matching cap sporting a gold and purple tassel. My husband was already in the car, equipped with his camera, feverishly emphasizing the need to leave early for a good parking spot. As we were all set to go, my younger daughter took a few moments to give her sister the warmest hug ever—the hug of joy, the hug of pride, and the hug of a sibling. The tears that streamed down their cheeks said it all—this was the beginning of their parting of ways, each one branching to a discipline of their choice, to lives of their own making, and to destinies ordained for them.

The commencement exercises were tastefully organized in the school auditorium, sheltering the parents and guests from the sizzling temperatures outside. As the guest speaker rose to speak, congratulating the new graduates, the words seem to trail away as my thoughts transported me to the day of my own graduation in India. I do not remember now who the speakers were, but a quote from one of them came alive:

If you carve on wood, they will crumble some day,
If you carve on stone, time will efface it,
But if you carve on the minds of the youth,
Imbuing them with spirit and a just fear of God,
Then you carve on something that will last through all
eternity.

How very true, I thought, now that I was a mother
with two girls of my own. There was still a lot of work
ahead, guiding teenage daughters through the mainstream of American culture. I was mentally back in the
auditorium now, trying to catch up with the concluding
remarks of the day. It was my turn to uninhibitedly shed
tears of joy as my daughter approached the podium to receive her diploma—her passport to ambitious beginnings.
My husband's camera captured the proud moments,
while his joy and hope remained ensconced in his castle of
confidence. A graduation party in the evening, complete
with banners, streamers, balloons, music, sumptuous
food and friends, marked the end of the celebrations. I
briefly mused over my last day in the Irish boarding
school in India. There were no commencement exercises,
no parties and no hoopla. All graduating seniors were
honored with silk shamrocks pinned onto our tunics by
Reverend Mother Principal as we filed past her in the
school auditorium. Teachers and dormitory staff hugged
us in tearful goodbyes. We were then escorted to the railway station to board our respective trains heading home.
My parents gave me a pat on the back for doing well and
told me to look forward to college in a couple of
months—it would be a college of their choice.
    The following year witnessed the graduation of our
younger daughter, calling for the same protocol, the same
location, and the same renewed identical moments of pa-

rental privilege. The girls were moving on to newer horizons that called for challenges and hitherto undemonstrated skills. As they got busy with their course work, I did likewise with my job.

America has always been known to be the country of doers, builders, and achievers—a leader in the industrialized world of today, the land of affluence where even the poorest of the poor could aspire for a decent meal. But beneath this fabric of apparent opulence, lay a grim dark world of ongoing need which I witnessed over the years in my job at the university. Bright, diligent students were not necessarily the wealthy ones, but their tight finances did not prevent them from sprinting towards the portals of a lucrative future. Meandering down memory lane, one incident comes to mind crystallizing with a clarity all its own. It was February of that year and in accordance with the Farmer's Almanac, the groundhog had seen his shadow indicating that six more weeks of winter were to follow. Awaiting onset of the ever-lovely spring had always been a welcome thought. Flowers and daffodils would make their debut in myriad hues, chirping of birds would announce the arrival of God's bountiful season, while waterways reckoned the melting of ice as renewing their communion with the fishing boats and yachts anchored in their bosom. It was as though Mother Nature took on a brush and palette each year, to bring alive the vibrant colors of her choice, dispelling the starkness of winter.

I was in my office, winding down for the day, when a student walked in—routinely as one of the many before him. He looked tired and famished and his large brown eyes exuded a sadness that I could not fathom in a soul of twenty-two summers. He inquired if there were any grant monies coming to him or any refunds at all, since he had run out of all resources and was now between a rock and a hard place. There were three more months to go before graduation. I pulled up his profile on the computer—indeed a consistently brilliant student now standing on the threshold of uncertainty with the harsh possibility of having to drop out. As I stared at the computer screen trying to deal with the wrenching pain within me, my mother's oft-quoted lines came to mind. It was from the Christian faith, she had said, and it ran thus:

> *On the street I saw a small girl*
> *Cold and shivering in a thin dress,*
> *With little hope of a decent meal.*
> *I became angry and said to God:*
> *Why did you permit this?*
> *Why don't You do something about it?*
>
> *For a while God said nothing.*
> *That night He replied quite suddenly:*
> *I certainly did something about it,*
> *I made you.*

I needed to think no further. I delved into my purse and wrote him a personal check to tide him over till graduation. Tears welled up in his eyes and his face became a study in expressions ranging from utter disbelief to immeasurable joy and lasting gratitude. His trembling hands accepted the check while his quivering lips spoke out, "Madam, I cannot thank you enough. How much time do I have to repay you?" I could sense him waiting with abated breath for my response. I escorted him to the door, assuring him that I expected no repayment whatsoever, but hoped that he would do likewise some day for a similarly worthy cause.

Three

Brahmoism, Hinduism and U.S. Citizenship

We had long met the requirements to become citizens of this country, and now decided to go through with the process of acquiring it. Our applications with the supporting documents were mailed out, and we were duly fingerprinted. We then waited our turn for the interview at the immigration and naturalization office in Buffalo, New York. It was a few months before we received the notification letter. We had, in the meantime, been updating ourselves with all the material relevant to the interview. It reminded me of the oral examinations in college at the post-graduate level. Although the scope here was very contained, the nervous and unsettled feelings were identical.

At the commencement of the interview, the INS officer—a trim, clean shaven gentleman with a graying mustache—placed me under oath to speak the truth and proceeded to ask me about my background and our current life in the U.S. He was all ears assessing the conversation while his eyes were deftly scanning my answers. Then came question time when he delved into the basics of American history. Here are a few highlights of what transpired:

Q: How many stripes are there on the U.S. Flag and what do they represent?

My Answer: Thirteen stripes representing the thirteen original states.

Q: What single word describes the supreme law of the land?
My Answer: The American Constitution.

The officer now seemed a trifle pleased, his demeanor being that of an examiner taking on a seemingly knowledgeable student.

Q: What is the national anthem of the U.S. and who wrote it?
My Answer: "The Star Spangled Banner" written by an obviously patriotic poet.

The officer had all along been making notations as I spoke. This time, however, he abruptly looked up at me with a cold, steely glance and an expression that seemed to say, *Lady, cut out the kidding.*

Q: How many stars are there on the U.S. flag and what do they represent?
My Answer: The stars represent the states of America, but as to the number, there is quite a cluster up there and I didn't really count.

The officer's exasperated look told me that I had goofed again. He decided to give me one more chance. "Stand up and take the Pledge of Allegiance," he said.

I knew I could expect no prompts from him. With my right hand on my heart, and my eyes fixed on the U.S. flag displayed alongside his table, I started, with a tremor in my voice:

"I pledge allegiance to the flag of the United States of America and to the Republic for which it stands—one nation under God, indivisible, with liberty and justice for all."

The officer was distinctly pleased and rose from his seat to congratulate me on a successful interview. He apprised me of my citizenship and that I would be notified by mail of the formal oath ceremony.

My husband's interview turned out to be routine, and our daughters acquired automatic citizenship since they were younger than eighteen years at the time. A fleeting element of nostalgia now reminded us that we had voluntarily surrendered our Indian citizenship with its rights and privileges, in order to wholly identify ourselves with the country of our choice.

The oath ceremony at the State Supreme Court in Syracuse was brief. All newly ordained citizens surrendered their "green cards" (permanent resident cards), took the Oath of Allegiance and received their Certificates of Naturalization. Facilities were also available in house to apply for the U.S. passport right away. Years later, when we undertook overseas vacation trips to different countries, we realized that possession of the U.S. passport accorded us welcome entries to most countries without the hassles of visas and entry permits.

My husband and I decided to avail a privilege of this newfound citizen status by sponsoring my widowed mother in India to join us here for the rest of her life. It would be months before she could arrive. Mother was the youngest daughter of one of Bengal's foremost leaders of the Nationalist Movement in India, in the first quarter of the twentieth century. She grew up at a time when the country was in the throes of a freedom movement, witnessing the toils and turmoil of a nation trying to unfetter itself from the shackles of British Imperialism. Born into a Hindu family, she was raised a "Brahmo," her father being one of the earliest disciples of Raja Ram Mohan Roy, who pioneered progress and reform in the then undivided India of the late 1800s.

Let me dip into a section of Indian history at this point, to explain the postulates of Brahmoism, in order for my readers to better appreciate the term "Brahmo." Brahmo Samaj initiated the first founding movement of social democracy in Bengal in mid 1800s. This led to the beginnings of emancipation and progress of the Bengali intelligentsia, the core doctrine of which demanded personal liberty and a monotheistic reformed view of Hinduism, the then prime practiced religion of the land. A new English-educated generation came into existence, intellectually contributing to progress in the true sense of the word, and supporting among other things, women's rights and education and widow re-marriage, while decrying idol worship, caste systems, the horrific practice of "Sati" (whereby a woman was expected to burn herself on the funeral pyre of her husband), and animal sacrifices.

The fundamental creed of the Brahmo doctrine in a nutshell is "God is One. From Brahman have all objects come into being; by Brahman all objects continue to be; toward Brahman all objects move through processes of cosmic evolution; and into Brahman all objects ultimately enter." (A quote from my grandfather, B. C. Pal—*My Life and Times,* Page 489.)

My mother who was convent-educated, articulate in English, and had the seeds of an activist ingrained in her, was given in marriage to a U.S. educated engineer in the 1920s. My father hailed from a conservative "Hindu" family of erstwhile East Bengal in undivided India. Let me pause here briefly to outline the basics of Hinduism as well, so that one can sense the combined religious climate in which I grew up.

Originating in the Indian sub-continent, Hinduism was the oldest, all-embracing, and tolerant religion, which also believed in a Supreme Cosmic Spirit called "Brahma," worshipped in many forms, represented by individual deities like Shiva and Vishnu. It revolved around many practices and rituals that were directed towards the ultimate realization of divinity. It was at this juncture that Hindus and Brahmos parted ways, since idol worship and related rituals were totally unacceptable to the Brahmos. Further, Hinduism entertained the caste system and considered the Vedas as the most sacred of Scriptures, while for the Brahmos, the "Brahmo Dharma" was a work of unique significance, extolling the principles of Brahmoism in the language of Vedas. Hindu temples were consecrated to specific deities, and temple honors done each day by a designated Brahmin priest to the chanting of "Slokas." In stark contrast, Brahmos congregated in spartan prayer halls from time to time. Their ministers known as "Acharyas" led the congregation. Commencing with invocation (Udbodhan), and followed by Brahmo Sangeets (hymns), the minister continued his sermon focusing on the Supreme, all-knowing, all-powerful, infinite, and formless God Almighty. The believers were urged in prayer to move on from darkness to light and from untruth to truth, desisting from the path of evil at all times. Brahmoism did not recognize any prophet, guru or priestly class as mediator between God and man.

32

The Brahmos celebrate "Maghotsav," their primary day-long festival in the month of Magh (January 22nd) of each year with prayers, singing of hymns, and a traditional vegetarian lunch consisting of kichudi (rice and lentils mix), vegetables and Bengali desserts. Their marriage ceremonies are usually registered and solemnized in the presence of their minister, along with the exchange of rings and garlands.

When I was born to my parents, they were way past their prime and at a stage of their lives when their differing religious thought processes had blended into a solidarity that made me consider religion as a progressive way of life and living. However, "Durga Puja"—a celebration of the homecoming of Goddess Durga—and "Diwali"—the festival of lights—were the two Hindu events we always participated in, every year. While on the subject, let me walk my readers through these two events and their religious injunctions. I remember visiting each year on "Ashtami morning" in the month of October, the festively decorated arena where the Durga Puja was being celebrated with bells and cymbals of tradition. The towering deity of Goddess Durga, attired in red, with all her splendor and mesmerizing beauty, was installed in a vantage position in the hall. Devotees dressed in their best, thronged in unceasingly with offerings of fruit and flowers and dedicated handmade sweets, the most popular being "Sandesh." After setting their offerings at the feet of the Goddess and bowing in prayer for their heart's desires, they receded to the rear of the hall for intermingling and socializing. Our presence at this function and our participation in the rituals were only to follow through on my father's Hindu upbringing and also to display my mother's culinary expertise in the art of making the delicious offering of "Sandesh." By all accounts, I was always more of an observer here watching the relentless gossip take off at jet pace. There was talk of the talented dancer-wife of a top shipping executive who eloped with the drummer of a performing group in town. Trying to make some sense of what I had just heard, I imagined that in the frenzy of drum dances, the dancer and the drum become an inseparable whirling unit and this art form was probably being enacted out in real life! Then there was the pretty, coy, socialite who decided overnight to become an activist of women's rights and eventually landed up behind bars.

The manor-born women offering to volunteer in the slums, tickets to regattas for boating enthusiasts, and news of high-end fashion stores in town were all topics of discussion regardless of the backdrop of religious fervor.

The uninterrupted chantings of the priest rent the air. Initial obeisance to the Goddess was offered in the "Pranam Mantra":

Om sarbamangala mangalye shibe sarbarthasadhike,
Sharanye trambake gouri narayani namastute

In English, it would translate thus:

Om, you are the provider of all benefits,
You are the most auspicious,
You are the perfect abode with three eyes,
You relate to Lord Narayana,
I bow down to thee.

The rituals continued at the feet of the deity amid lighted lamps and incense sticks and so did the socializing at the far end of the hall. Shortly before noon, announcements over the PA system advised the gathering that the final offering of "Pushpanjali," salutation with flowers to the Goddess would commence shortly and urged all participating devotees to assemble in front of the deity. The next few minutes saw total compliance while little trays of flower petals were passed around to the congregation.

The presiding priests commenced chanting the "Mantras,"

Oh divine great mother,
You are apparently ferocious but truly benevolent,
You bestow upon us long life and victory over evil,
I bow down to thee who relates to Lord Narayana,
And offer this flower smeared with sandalwood paste.

While we remembered to hold onto our flower petals until the rendering of the chantings was complete, the priests continued:

You are the eternal force behind creation, sustenance and destruction,
The ultimate abode of the three Gunas: Sathva, Rajas and Tamas,
And you comprise all three of them,
I bow down to thee who relates to Lord Narayana
And offer this flower smeared with sandalwood paste.

And now, the concluding mantra before we showered the flower petals at the feet of the deity:

Om sharanagata deenarta paritranaparayane,
Sarbasyartri hare devi Narayani namastute,
Esha sachandana pushpanjali om dakshayogya,
Vinashinoyee mahaghorai yogini kotiparibritaoi,
Bhadrakalyoee hring om durgaoyee nama:

35

This would translate as follows:

You are the constant saviour of those
Who surrender to you in poverty and suffering;
You are the remover of all distress:
I bow down to thee who relates to Lord Narayana,
And offer this flower smeared with sandalwood paste.

At this point the crowds lunged forward to shower the flower petals at the feet of the Goddess, confiding their innermost aspirations to her one more time, while I on my part prayed for insight and wisdom to be able to view all faiths with equal candor and regard. The sea of human faces now headed towards the dining hall where "Prashad," a sanctified offering of fruits and milk pudding, was being distributed, to be followed by a sumptuous vegetarian lunch consisting of: khichudi (rice and lentils), luchi (fried puffed flat bread), chanar dalna (cheese ball curry), phoolkopir dalna (cauliflower delicacy), sweet chutney and a range of irresistable Bengali desserts.

On this auspicious eighth day of rituals, Goddess Durga is believed to have triumphed over demon Mahishasura. The next day, Navami, is dedicated to ultimate salutations to the Goddess. On the tenth and final day known as Dashami, the deity is immersed in the ocean symbolizing her return to her consort's abode, while devotees fervently await her return at the same time each year.

Diwali was the other event that we never failed to observe. Acquiring its name from the rows of little glittering clay oil lamps called "Diyas" that adorn the homes during the dark fortnight in the Hindu month of Ashwin (Octo-

36

ber–November), this "Festival of Lights" is symbolically believed to dispel darkness and impart knowledge and self-realization. The sights and sounds of the firecrackers rocketing into the skies announce the commencement of the celebrations. Homes are decorated with mango leaves and marigolds, while artistic "Rangolis" are drawn on the front courtyards with colored powders in traditional motifs considered auspicious symbols of good luck.

The ancient story of how Diwali evolved into such a widely celebrated festival, varies with the different regions in India. In the North, it is the day when King Rama's victory and coronation were celebrated after his epic war with Ravana, the demon king of Sri Lanka, according to the epic *Ramayana*. Essentially, it conveyed the triumph of good over evil. In the South, the festival commemorates the conquering of the demon "Narakashura" by Lord Krishna. Here again, lighted clay lamps adorn the homes, sometimes flickering in obeisance to the passing breeze, while the firecrackers zoom upwards briefly illuminating their skyward journey. Fresh flowers, new clothes, traditional sweets and an air of festivity sum up the celebratory fervor.

In Bengal, Kali puja coincides with the Diwali festival, the only difference being while the rest of India at this time invokes Lakshmi, the Goddess of Wealth, the chief deity venerated here is Kali, the aggressive form of Goddess Durga. Celebrations are similar and devotees seek blessings of happiness, prosperity and health.

Whatever the legends behind the Diwali celebration, the universally observed feature of the event is indulging in sweets and wearing new apparel in a spirit of festive gaiety. In America, our hometown sported a large ethnic Indian community where these events held a significant place in the calendar of festivals. Erudite religious scholars, not withstanding their chosen professions in the U.S., conducted the religious rituals in rented halls. In recent times however, officiating Hindu priests have become more readily available.

The Festival of Lights is observed here in a more subdued fashion, in deference to the "fire code" regulations. Decorative candles illuminate the hearths and homes while Indian caterers have field days marketing traditional Indian sweets. And there never is a dearth of garment stores, as always.

Four

Arrival of My Mother

It was a good six months before my mother got her visa to come to the United States and I made a hurried trip to India to escort her back. Tiny in stature to begin with, she looked even more frail to me, but her towering principles and indomitable will prevailed. Before boarding the flight in India, she looked around her, briefly seeming to be immersed in thoughts of her own, while her eyes welled up with tears. She soon regained her self-control and a sense of realism took over as she prepared for boarding formalities. I knew she was recalling her cherished fifty years of wedded life with my father in the land of her birth, his passing away and the void she had endured ever since. She was also aware of the prospect of her never being able to set foot again on her beloved native soil in view of her failing health. The flight crew waited on her with special attention, especially because of her age. In-flight movies did not interest her, nor did the newspapers and magazines. She did not rest her eyes throughout the flight, possibly for fear of being dropped off in the wrong country! As the jumbo jet came in to land at New York, her face lit up like never before with an obvious anticipation in her countenance. Her longing to hold her two beloved granddaughters in her arms became at once apparent. The sentiments were reciprocal as the girls rushed to savor this long awaited moment of reunion with Grandma, hugging in the process the wheelchair as well! Her son-in-law was the last to be noticed in the frenzy. As we walked alongside her, I noticed she was taking in everything she saw around her. At one point, she turned to me and said, "Tell me one thing. I see so many restrooms in this airport, but no toilets at all. Do people here like to rest up ever so often?" I was struck by her simple, naïve interpretation and hastened to explain that "restrooms" and "toilets" were one and the same.

Adapting to the Western way of life was never an issue for her, though she very much held her own when it came to a compromise of values that she was raised with. She was always an early riser, and the initial jet lag bothered her when she found herself falling asleep during the day. In a week, however, she was back on normal schedule. Her mornings were spent assisting with breakfast and the rest of the day planning and fixing dinner. Her mouthwatering dishes incorporated freshly ground spices like coriander, cumin, mustard, and turmeric along with cardamom, cinnamon and cloves for their fragrance. To me, it was Indian luxury revisited. While serving tea or coffee to guests, she made sure sugar and cream came in their respective containers unlike in India where beverages were served with all ingredients appropriately blended. She learned to greet our Caucasian friends with a handshake, while it was invariably a traditional "Namaste" with all others.

She, for some reason, had always dreaded having her toenails clipped and only the doctors in the family were entitled to do the honors. She insisted that she was granting them the special privilege! Her independent spirit invariably carried a silver lining of reality. She watched television at times but abruptly turned it off if the media reported too much violence. Graciousness and hospitality were her hallmarks. In time she came to be affectionately known as "Mashima" (aunty) or "Dida" (grandmother) to all our friends. At informal parties, friends enjoyed Grandma's homemade dishes, and she never failed to tell them each time, "Remember me by my cooking when I pass on."

To my mother, her precious granddaughters could do no wrong. If they came home past the curfew hour, she forthwith came up with a reason—they were studying hard, fatigued after a long day of classes, and the cautious girls drove home within the speed limit.

At the end of five years of her stay in the U.S., we one day casually apprised her of her rights to U.S. citizenship. She retaliated like a wounded lioness. "Don't you ever forget my heritage or my lineage. Patriotic blood still runs strong in my veins and I will remain Indian to my last breath. And don't ever bring this topic up again." Having said that, she walked to her room, while we sat dumbfounded, wondering what we had said so offensive.

Before long she returned with an envelope in her hands. Slowly and deliberately she took out its contents—a First Day Cover imprinted with her father's picture and a postage stamp issued by the Government of India in commemoration of his birth centenary. Her lips quivering with emotion, she said, "I don't have an estate to leave behind for you, but I am leaving a legacy that you can always cherish with pride." She handed us the cover and stamp which we treasure to this day.

My mother lived for seven more years with us, participating in her granddaughters' wedding celebrations as well. When asked if she had any particular unfulfilled wish, she would shake her head and say, "No, I have lived a full life. However, when my end comes, allow me to die at home with my loved ones at my side. No heroic measures or respirators, please." She had picked up many

"Birth Centennial First Day Cover" of author's grandfather

medical terminologies over the years here. A month before Halloween, in 1992, she slipped into a coma. Round-the-clock nursing service was arranged at home, in accordance with her wishes, and on Halloween day, with all of us at her bedside, she breathed her last. A memorial service and prayers were conducted at our home after the stipulated thirteen days, followed by a meal consisting of her favorite dishes. The officiating priest, a senior educationist and friend, spoke about the eternity of the soul, that birth was the union of the soul with the body and death the separation from it. He exhorted the grieving family to consider Death as yet another phase of Life and that mortals should through their good deeds and actions in successive rebirths, aim for the ultimate salvation. This, he said, translates to being freed from the cycle of births and deaths and realization of the Supreme Divinity. To me, my mother had always been a rock of

42

support, a haven of solace, a pillar of strength, and her weathered life a treasure hut of wisdom. To the world she might have been just another person, but to me she was the world.

Five

Indian Wedding on Yankee Soil

Robert Frost in his poem "Stopping by Woods on a Snowy Evening" had written:

The woods are lovely, dark and deep,
But I have promises to keep,
And miles to go before I sleep,
And miles to go before I sleep.

So true indeed. It was not yet time for us to rest. The children's marriages had to be arranged, suitable grooms to be found and weddings solemnized in Indian tradition. Was I dreaming overtime and were my thoughts sprinting in leaps and bounds into improbable terrain? Only time would tell.

The procedural practice of a Hindu marriage normally runs along the following guidelines:

1. Parents hear about prospective brides and grooms through friends and relatives, through marriage brokers who carry a list of eligible candidates complete with family backgrounds, and lately there have been established matrimonial bureaus for the purpose.

2. The next step is bride viewing. After a thorough background search, the groom with his parents and a few elders visits the home of the possible bride. The coy bride

is the focus of the evening. She is assessed from head to toe based on her looks, her qualifications, her likes and dislikes, and her domestic inclinations. If duly impressed, the groom's family partake in the snacks and drinks served on the occasion. Otherwise they leave, promising to convey their decision by messenger or mail.

3. In the event of moving ahead with a positive alliance, the next crucial step calls for matching of the horoscopes of the bride and the groom. Under the Hindu predictive systems, astrological compatibility is believed to indicate the likely positive and negative features of the couple's health, wealth, longevity and progeny. Given the precise dates and times of their birth, the horoscopes are drawn up based on the positions of the celestial bodies which in turn are governed by the planetary influences of Saturn, Jupiter, Mars, Venus, Mercury, Uranus, Neptune, Sun and Moon. At the conclusion of all these procedures involving heaven and earth, a wedding date is finally set.

I was, in no form or fashion, prepared to adhere to all these traditional formats. All I wanted was to reserve the option of suggesting compatible grooms for matrimonial consideration.

Our younger daughter, Shoba, had just graduated from engineering school in our prestigious hometown university, when I sat her down to one of those intimate mother-daughter discussions.

I gently talked her into giving me the clearance to look for a suitable groom. I did realize that she had, by now, definitive opinions on marriage and career. To her, the words "arranged marriage" seemed to convey some sort of established indignity. I spent days trying to bridge the obvious cultural and generational gap. I explained to her that the apparently objectionable term "arranged" was not really intended to shut out all other possibilities. It was only opening up the doors for more options, given the discretion, wisdom, and experience of the family elders. Shoba finally agreed, setting down some conditions of her own. The groom had to be handsome, be able to speak English without an accent, and wear pleated pants and pointed shoes. *That wasn't such a tall order,* I told myself. My husband added his preferences to the list—a doctor or a professional at the very least. My mother, not to be left behind, said in soft undertones, "Make sure he is from a good family."

Eligible grooms in India were located by word of mouth, and I made the momentous trip, holding my daughter's future in my hands, as it were. The prospective groom fulfilled the ambitious requirements on our list—down to the pointed shoes. More importantly, his parents were educated, genuine, caring people who swept me off my feet at the very first meeting. I secretly hoped that I did likewise. I flew back to the U.S. to present my case to my daughter who would be both judge and jury in making the decision.

Favorably impressed with what she saw on the video-tape, she decided to visit them in India on a week's vacation. The groom fell head over heels for her, and his parents approved wholeheartedly. Rather than wait for six months to conduct an elaborate wedding in India, it was decided that the couple get married in the next few days. This would enable the groom to come to the U.S. faster and prepare for his qualifying examinations and residency. A brief wedding was duly solemnized as per the Hindu rites, followed by an endorsement by the marriage registrar. The rituals were kept short in view of the time constraint. The bride and groom, in their wedding attires, were led to the consecrated fireplace where Vedic mantras were being chanted by the priest. The groom then tied the "Mangalsutra" or the auspicious chain around the bride's neck with "Agni," the God of Fire, as witness. Together the couple prayed for long life, progress, prosperity and harmony. Following this was the important ritual of "Saptapadi" when they took seven steps around the fire invoking God's blessings for a blissful married life. The assembled guests then blessed the couple and participated in the wedding feast.

Our daughter, on her return home, filed the sponsorship papers without delay, and in two months the groom was winging his way to the U.S. On the appointed day of his arrival in New York, my husband and Shoba positioned themselves at a vantage point in the visitors' area of the airport, all set to welcome him home. The flight landed and the passengers walked out followed by the flight crew. But the groom was nowhere to be seen. Anxiety was mounting, when the nervous bride declared, "Oh! There he is!" My husband's eyes turned to the gentleman she pointed out. He was shocked to see a man who looked much older, had a potbelly but bore some resemblance to the groom. Thankfully he happened to be somebody else. The anxiety had now gotten to my husband as well. He rushed to the nearest telephone to tell me that the new bride was not sure whom she married! Mounting tension now pervaded us at home as well, till the phone rang again with good tidings this time—the groom had finally arrived after a delay in immigration. Over the years, it became obvious that a better choice could not have been made on both ends of the marriage spectrum.

Our older daughter, Nita, had by now met the "beau of her dreams" in medical school. He was a tall, handsome young man with a charisma all his own, raised in the U.S. and hailing from an eminent Brahmin family of South India. As is customary, the families met and a date was set for the wedding the following year at Sri Venkateshwara Temple in Pittsburgh, Pennsylvania. The ceremony was to be followed by a reception in Syracuse. Conducting a traditional Indian wedding on Yankee soil was not going to be a piece of cake, I realized. More so since I was a Bengali with scant knowledge of South Indian rituals. Challenges in life had never demoralized me, and I was not going to let it happen now.

Working in conjunction with the groom's mother who was a lady with tremendous foresight, capability, and more importantly an abiding sense of finesse, I figured out the South Indian luncheon menu and the wedding rituals as well. The local caterer for Indian weddings in Pittsburgh came highly recommended and assured us that the dishes would be of the highest standards. With a sizable advance deposit, the deal was clinched. A month ahead of the wedding, preparations set in with feverish activity. The telephones were ringing off the hook with calls from the hotel, the temple, and various other vendors, but strangely none from the caterer. An eerie sense of uneasiness befell me and a couple of days before the event, I decided to call them in Pittsburgh. A young male voice responded at the other end. He informed me very casually that his mother, the designated cook, had gone to India on a two-month vacation. My mouth instantly went parch-dry and my trembling fingers could hardly hold on to the receiver. With a barely audible gasp I asked, "What happens to the catering now?"

Seemingly unperturbed he replied, "My father and I

can handle it. I can fix that sticky, gooey dessert called 'Piyaaasam' (correctly pronounced as Payasam), and father can try his hand at the main courses."

By now, my knees were trembling and my head reeling with a feel of impending blackout. Enraged, I could only blurt out, "Cancel this contract right now." I slumped into the nearest sofa, unable to think rationally anymore. Only three days to the wedding and a horrendous letdown by the caterer. From the innermost depths of my heart, I prayed to God for help out of this abyss of catastrophe. Just about then, a friend of a friend residing in Pittsburgh called, offering help with the wedding arrangements. On hearing my predicament, she suggested a very experienced local culinary expert but the issue was—would they undertake a catering contract of this magnitude at such a short notice? I died a thousand deaths waiting for the phone call of my life. Within the hour I was informed that the response was "yes." To me, undoubtedly, this had to be Divine intervention.

The preparations for the wedding were carefully orchestrated in keeping with the Hindu traditions of South India. Requests from the bridal couple to keep the ceremony as short as possible fell on deaf ears since every ritual was meant for an auspicious outcome. Any willful omission might well annoy the gods or the stars!

The evening before the wedding, the activities seemed to rise to a hitherto unseen crescendo. Friends decorated the wedding arena with yards of silk flowers and fresh flower pots, while others were busy stringing red and white carnation garlands for the couple. A cuisine savvy panel supervised luncheon arrangements. My husband, sporting a secure leather bag containing the bride's jewelry and other valuables, periodically showed up to enforce his presence, and our younger son-in-law who was the "senior son-in-law" for the day, literally carried on his shoulders the responsibility of seeing the event to a smooth conclusion. The physical presence of the caterers was like soothing balm to my jittery nerves. To the groom and the bride in their respective hotels, the morrow would probably be yet another day in their lives, while they dwelt on possible residency positions in hospitals of their choices. The auspicious day had dawned. Designated ladies decked the bride in traditional wedding attire, with the jewelry and brocade sari competing to outdo each other. Amidst the heightened hustle and bustle, amidst last minute consultations with elders of the groom's family, amidst being smack in the middle of all the goings on, part of me continued to endure the gnawing tinge of pain that only the mother of a bride could feel. From this day on, my "little girl" would belong to another family. The silent tears were persistent in overflowing the brim, and I made no attempt to stop them. Wasn't I entitled to these moments as a mother, I asked myself? A little voice from within responded, "Yes, but not for long."

The Hindu marriage is viewed as a sacrament, a divine sanctity and a lifelong commitment between man and woman. The marriage rites, comprising of relevant "poojas" or ceremonies performed under a festively decorated "mandap" or canopy, are believed to spiritually unite two souls in harmony. The invitees to the wedding started arriving punctually, were received at the entrance with sprinkling of rose water, anointed with sandal paste, offered fresh flowers and escorted to their seats in the wedding hall. Traditional "Nadaswaram" music was being played in the background. Nadaswaram is a wind instrument similar to the "Shehnai" and played on auspicious occasions. The priest, seated under the canopy, commenced chanting the intial invocations with the resounding word "Om." As per the Upanishads, Om is the imperishable syllable. Om is the universe, the past, the present and the future. All that was, all that is and all that will be is Om. All else that may exist beyond the bounds of time, too is Om.

WELCOMING THE GROOM: The groom, representing an embodiment of Lord Vishnu, arrived with his family to the chanting of a hymn sung in the glory of Lord Narayana. We, the parents of the bride, welcomed them and led the groom to the "mandap."

VRATHAM: The marriage rites began with the vratham, performed ahead individually by the bride and the groom. For the bride, it involved tying of the holy thread on her wrist to ward off evil spirits. For the groom, the vratham began with invocation of the Gods: Indra, Soma, Chandra and Agni. From this point on he was to prepare himself for the impending new phase of his life as a "grihasta," bidding farewell to bachelorhood.

GANAPATI POOJA: The priest entreated Lord Ganesha, remover of obstacles, to keep away all impediments and avert all obstacles so that the ceremony and the couple's married life may proceed smoothly and peacefully.

NAVAGRAHA POOJA: Nine planets that govern our destinies were invoked to ensure that they shower their choicest blessings upon the couple.

KASHI YATRA: This is a symbolic ritual at this point, when the groom supposedly heads to the religious town of Kashi, donning the garb of a hermit, complete with umbrella, slippers and a bamboo fan. A few yards into this journey my husband in his role as the bride's father had to stop him, promising to give him our daughter in marriage and advocating the superiority of married life over renunciation.

We then ceremoniously escorted the groom into the wedding arena, washed his feet with milk, wiped them with silk and led him to the canopy.

ARRIVAL OF THE BRIDE: While the groom waited under the canopy with a white curtain held in front of him as a symbolic barrier, our daughter the bride arrived, escorted by her sister and friends, to the chanting of hymns sung in praise of "Devi" the Goddess. The white curtain was now removed and the bride and groom exchanged flower garlands thrice to signify their union as one soul in two bodies. They then joined hands in acceptance of each other and the willingness to go through life together, in good times and bad. We then led the couple to the nearby swing and as they sat on it, rocking back and forth, designated women sang songs in their praise. We took handfuls of colored rice, waved it in front of them in a circular motion and discarded it in order to ward off the evil spirits.

KANYAADAN: Presentation of the Bride.

Our daughter was now seated on her father's lap to be given away in marriage to the groom. On her head was placed a dried grass ring over which sat a symbolic yoke holding the "Mangalsutra"—a gold chain entwined with turmeric coated thread and carrying a traditional gold pendant. Sprinkling water over the yoke, the priest chanted:

Let this gold multiply your wealth,
Let this water purify your married life,
May your prosperity increase,
Offer yourself to your husband.

MAANGALYA DHARANAM: This was the most auspicious and awaited moment of the marriage ceremony.

To the loud and fast beat of music, made deliberately deafening so as to muffle any inauspicious sounds at the critical hour, the groom placed the "Mangalsutra" chain on our daughter's neck, assisted by his sisters. The audience now blessed the couple by tossing yellow rice and flower petals on them.

PAANI GRAHANAM: Joining of Hands.

The groom then held our daughter's hands as corners of her sari and the groom's shawl were tied together to seal the pact. The mantras chanted translated into: "The Gods have offered you to me in order that I may live the life of a grihasta and shall we not part from each other even as we grow old."

SAPTAPADHI: The Seven Steps.

This very significant ritual, without which the ceremony is not complete, consisted of the couple taking seven steps together around the holy fire as the priest recited the mantras. Each step signified a vow in the presence of "Agni," the God of Fire. The seven vows were:

1. Shall we be true companions and inseparable friends for ever.
2. Shall we share eternal love for each other.
3. Shall we share the same food and nourish each other.
4. Shall we share in our physical, mental and spiritual strength.
5. Shall we help and serve others.
6. Shall we create a happy and healthy family together.
7. Shall we acquire knowledge, happiness and harmony through mutual love and trust.

PRADHANA HOMAM: Homage to "Agni," God of Fire.

This important part of the marriage rites involved the couple performing the homam, using clarified butter and twigs from nine types of trees, as sacrificial fuel. The fumes arising are believed to be medicinal, curative and cleansing for the couple. Agni, the mightiest power in the Cosmos, the sacred purifier, the omnipresent benefactor, was thus deemed witness to the marriage.

SILAROHANA: Treading on the grindstone.

Our daughter was helped onto the grindstone as the mantras were chanted: "Mount on this stone. Let thy mind be rock firm, unperturbed by the trials and tribulations of life." At this time, the groom stooped to place silver toe rings on her feet. In a lighter vein, it seemed to me that he was essentially "stooping to conquer."

VIEWING THE ARUNDHATI STAR: The couple then stepped outdoors when the groom was asked to point out to our daughter the star "Arundhati," also known as "Polaris." Arundhati, the wife of sage Vasishta, had been exemplified as an ideal wife and the embodiment of chastity.

LAAJA HOMAM: Is a ritual where a brother or similarly placed cousin of our daughter assisted the couple in offering rice grains to the fire. Through this offering, Nita was seeking a long life for her husband and their family. The participation of a brother signified the continuing link between the two families.

AASHIRWAD: Blessing. The ceremony concluded with more saffron rice and flower petals being showered on the newlyweds by the priests, the elders, and the audience.

The wedding ceremony was followed by a sumptuous vegetarian lunch which drew acclaims from even established connoisseurs of South Indian cooking, reaffirming my unshaken faith in the Supreme Power through the most testing times.

A reception ensued in our hometown, after which life gravitated to a normalcy in the next few weeks. Both our daughters, seasoned young ladies now, returned to their careers. Years of toil and commitment took Nita, the physician, to positions of recognition, while intellectual and people skills helped Shoba, the engineer, up the corporate ladder.

Many of our Western friends were curious as to why I had not opted for a Bengali wedding for our daughters. The primary reason for that was the fact that my husband as well as the prospective grooms hailed from the same state in Southern India. And, as always, the majority prevailed. Further, I found most Hindu wedding rituals to be very similar with slight variations from state to state. They all encompass the core Vedic tenets, highlighted by the following major ceremonies:

Ganesh Puja—Invoking Lord Ganesh.
Agni Puja—Evoking the holy fire.
Kanyadana—Giving away the bride to the groom.
Mangalsutra—Tying of holy necklace.
Saptapadi—The Seven Steps circling the holy fire.
Silarohana—Bride steps on the stone.

In a traditional Bengali wedding, the bridegroom and his entourage arrive at the wedding arena (invariably the bride's home) and are duly welcomed with ceremonial honors by the bride's mother. The groom then takes his place on the wedding altar under the traditional canopy, sporting a white headgear called "Topor." The bride, anointed earlier with turmeric and decked in red bridal attire complete with a similar headgear called "Mukut," is made to sit on a low stool and lifted up by her brothers to circle seven times round the groom. While still hoisted up on the shoulders of her brothers, the bride and groom exchange flower garlands thrice. Back to the canopy the bride's father gives her hand in marriage to the groom amidst chanting of mantras by the priest. With enjoined hands, they touch the "Mangalghot"—a brass pitcher of water adorned with mango leaves over which sits a green coconut. As the ceremony proceeds the couple go round the holy fire seven times, acknowledging "Agni" the God of Fire, as the divine witness to the marriage. The ceremony concludes with the bride's brother handing puffed rice to the couple who then jointly feed it into the fire.

Bengali weddings, however, are incomplete without "Sindoor Daan" when the groom applies Sindoor or vermilion on the bride's hair parting and she is expected to keep it up as long as he lives.

Six

New Lease on Life
for a Young Medico

Some people come into our lives briefly and move on but some leave indelible imprints in our hearts, as Nithya did.

It was a bright October morning in 1989. The autumn foliage in shades of yellow, orange and brown interspersed with patches of lazy green could easily beckon a Nature's artist into its folds. Pinecones high up in the branches had decided to move to lower ground in the hope of making their way into festive Christmas wreaths. As I idled around sipping a cup of coffee and viewing the undefied glory of the changing seasons, I decided to browse through the recent edition of a popular Indian newspaper. There was nothing particular on the first few pages that would set my pulse racing, till my eyes fell on this lengthy ad—an appeal, to be more precise. The caption read "Give her a new lease on life." We see such ads for help routinely, but somehow this one seemed to be different. My curiosity egged me to read on: a brilliant young medico had been fighting the most debilitating odds since birth, surviving on a single kidney and diverted urinary tract. Raging fevers, excruciating pain and a social stigma had become a way of life for her. Regardless, she had made tremendous strides with a remarkable patience in one so young, nurturing an undying hope of survival and a near-normal life.

The existing diversion had run into multiple complications, seriously threatening her only kidney. She needed a rare life-saving operation in the U.S.A.—a state of the art surgery which however came with no guarantees or assurances. The finances for a surgery of this magnitude in this country were very steep. While the eminent surgeon was prepared to render his services pro bono, contributions in dollars were needed and needed urgently to cover ICU and hospitalization charges. When I was done reading this emotionally charged appeal, my thoughts instantly sprinted to my mother's oft-quoted verse from the Christian faith when God's indifference to human suffering is questioned and He replies "I certainly did something about it. I made you."

I knew very well that it was beyond me to deal single-handedly with this situation. My husband and I sent in our humble contribution toward the surgery, but that was the easy part. A restlessness continued to rage deep within me projecting the vicissitudes of her condition, the possible fallibilities of surgical expertise and what price, if any, fate would claim to placate ruthless morbidity.

A week before her surgery, the young medico arrived in the U.S. and wasted no time communicating with us on the telephone. At that point, I asked her if there was anything, anything at all that we could do for her. In a hesitating, faltering voice she replied that nothing would make her happier than to be able to see us in person by her bedside when she was wheeled into surgery. Her request called for a 600 mile commute to Norfolk, Virginia, where the world's renowned urologists were engaged in innovative surgery. The next few days saw us preparing for the trip. The huge imposing hospital seemed to be the "Mecca" of the sickest and the hopeful. We saw attending physicians with retinues of medical students on teaching rounds, residents hastening to answer their pages, and trauma teams waiting to receive the screeching ambulances. The buzz of activity was ongoing.

From the front desk we were directed to the surgical floor where we were going to set eyes for the first time on this challenged crusader who had left no stone unturned in her quest for life and a dignified existence. We paused at the entrance to her room—all we could see was a frail figure clutching a Teddy on the bed, from where originated tangles of tubings and IV bottles. As we got closer, she turned towards us with outstretched arms of welcome, as though savoring a long-lost relationship. No formal introductions were needed. Those few electrifying moments defied all bonds of genetics, all barriers of caste, creed and religion. We had now acquired a new daughter! Tears streamed down her cheeks as well as mine, while little rivulets of water cascaded down the faces of her parents.

Her fourteen-hour surgery commenced the next morning, followed by a lengthy ICU recovery. Her surgeon was cautiously optimistic, and a month later declared her fit for discharge, given that she remained in the U.S. for the next six months for close monitoring. Our newly acquired daughter came home to us and we had the privilege of her company until she went back to India. She however returned shortly to train in the U.S. and is now an eminent oncologist in this country, happily married to a trauma surgeon. We see them on a regular basis, and each passing year serves to strengthen the bonds of closeness.

Over the years, chance encounters led us to people, young and old, in varying forms of distress—some needing a shoulder to cry on, some needing a roof over their heads till they found themselves, and some needing a renewed vote of confidence in their own capabilities before they dared to step out into the real world. There were others for whom a few hours of company at their hospital bedsides meant the world to them, folks struggling to understand and be understood in a foreign country with little knowledge of English to fall back on. Their toothless smiles and tear-filled eyes as they gently squeezed my hands in appreciation, were towering tributes to a little person like me. I can recall to this day the one common characteristic that shone like a beacon light through their life of travails—their enduring love to this day as it was then. To me, that is the most coveted medallion of honor that one mortal could bestow on another. I do believe that one has to be extremely fortunate and privileged to be able to appreciate the unfolding beauty and joy in the multifaceted world of giving—giving without condescension, giving without fanfare and giving without hurting human dignity.

Ralph Waldo Emerson in his poem "Success" had said:

"To leave the world a bit better whether by a healthy child, a garden patch, or a redeemed social condition; to know even one life has breathed easier because you have lived. This is to have succeeded."

Part II

Travels

*For my vicarious readers who would like to see
the world from the comfort of their armchairs*

Seven

Australia and New Zealand—February 1993

With both our daughters married and settled in their respective careers and with my mother having passed on,
we decided to travel to different countries and discover
new cultures—entering a global classroom, so to say. We
wanted to gain an in-depth understanding of people, their
heritages and thought processes. To my husband, it was a
form of continuing education and enlightenment through
firsthand observations. To me, it was that and more—an
inexplicable schoolgirl euphoria of seeing a cherished
dream come true. Were we expecting our travel experiences to influence our inner beings and our spirituality
over the years? Well, that was left to be seen. In this con-
text, however, poet Rabindranath Tagore's lines from
"Gitanjali" come to mind:

> *The traveler has to knock*
> *at every alien door*
> *to come to his own,*
> *and he has to wander*
> *through all the outer worlds*
> *to reach the innermost shrine at the end.*

Being first-time entrants in the world of travel and
tourism, we commenced by reading relevant books, talk-
ing to friends who were inspired travelers, assessing the

duration and nature of the trip in keeping with our own endurance levels, and lastly determining an affordable budget. Seeking a two-week getaway from the harsh winters of the northeast, we decided on Australia and New Zealand where summer reigns from December through March. The all-inclusive package on an "escorted" tour, with reputed travel professionals, promised "garden-view rooms" at high-end hotels, feather beds and down comforters, marble baths, cuisines to remember and service at a personal level. The inviting sounds of it had us making quick decisions and before long, necessary travel documents, airline tickets and welcome packages were sent to us by courier service. A close look at the itinerary clearly indicated that we were going to be on a "school bus" schedule, boarding the tourist motor coaches at the stroke of eight in the morning and returning by sunset. Walking shoes were a must as also the suggested clothing. Acceptable levels of fitness to deal with high-paced rigors of the trip were not particularly addressed, just like ad disclaimers in fine print!

In February 1993, we boarded a fourteen-hour nonstop flight from Los Angeles to Sydney. We were twenty people in the travel group and landed in Australia pretty tired but with excitement clearly stamped on our countenances. We were briefed in the hotel lounge on the day's itinerary—it was to be a day of rest and leisure, followed by a formal welcome dinner in the evening when subsequent briefings would take place. The rooms were as promised and the service was superb. The elegant evening dinner helped to essentially promote socializing within our travel group.

My ethnic "sari" drew raving compliments on the combination of colors, the sheen and softness of the silk, and the overall draping style. Some enterprising ladies requested a sari draping demonstration right there, if possible. I promised them a session at some point during the trip, when partial disrobing could be done in privacy. However, I proceeded to educate them on this form of attire which has been the Indian woman's fashion statement to the world from time immemorial.

The classic form of the sari is six yards of unstitched material, ranging from shimmering silks to fine cottons, psychedelic colors to attractive prints, or featuring a gold thread weave for the brocade look. It is draped differently in different states of India in keeping with the diversity of the Indian people. The nine-yard version of it is more cumbersome but still used in some states by conservative women. I wonder if the American expression "going the whole nine yards" had its origin in the involved and time-consuming format of this style. Interesting questions were raised, most of which centered around understandable concerns of the sari holding up indefinitely and the possibility of it falling apart at the slightest tug, much to the embarrassment of the wearer. The Sari 101 class ended with my concluding statement: "Friends, as in any other discipline, with experience comes expertise and with expertise comes perfection." We were off to a great start in a new country with our cosmopolitan trip mates.

The highlights of the next few days were visits to:

1. The Opera House in Sydney.
2. The trek to the summit of Sydney Harbor Bridge.
3. The Taronga Zoo.
4. A sunset dinner cruise.
5. A day trip to nearby Manly Island.

We would have leisure time for shopping as schedules permitted.

The Opera House, situated in an idyllic location off the Sydney Harbor, is an all-time marvel of contemporary architecture. We spent hours there soaking up its stunning beauty and witnessing its unseen workings. It is undoubtedly one of the most awesome performing art venues of the world.

After a short break for lunch, we were on our way to the Sydney Harbor Bridge, bracing ourselves for the climb to the summit which, we were told, was a sought-after tourist attraction. In hindsight, a few days of physical endurance training might have helped. The trek on catwalks and ladders, at a height of 400 feet above the ocean, left us panting, gasping and inordinately thirsty. The breathtaking view of the sprawling city from up there, the azure ocean beneath, the majestic mountains in the rear and the clear blue skies above, gave us the kind of euphoria that Sir Edmund Hillary and Tensing Norgay must have experienced on the peak of Mount Everest. The downward return was comparatively a breeze and once on level ground, we lost no time calling it a day and hastily walked towards the motor coach that was to take us back to the hotel. We were weary and exhausted and after a hurried dinner with our equally tired peers, we retired for the night, instantly welcoming the slumber as our head hit the pillows.

The next morning at the stroke of eight, we were again in our motor coach headed to the famous Taronga Zoo which was located on a hillside overlooking the Sydney Harbor. It was captivating to see native animals like the wombats and emus, elephants and giraffes at close quarters, incredibly cute red pandas, wallabies, gorillas and koalas and the hopping kangaroos with their little ones in their pouches. Some of them paused to look at us briefly in the eye. The spring in their step and their incessant hurry to get to nowhere was their enduring appeal. To me, the Chilean flamingoes with their signature "peach and white" hues, were the most inspiring—some displaying their plumes in a single leg stand, others seemingly absorbed in training sessions with their young ones, and yet others vacantly gazing on with an undulating grace all their own. The penguins came a close second, waddling in a little colony at their own measured pace, and unmindful of the world of tourists fleeting past them.

Back to the hotel for a lunch and siesta, we rested up while outdoor enthusiasts chose other activities of their liking.

The sunset dinner cruise on Sydney Harbor was undoubtedly an evening to remember. With reserved window seats in the cruising restaurant, we had two hours to relish gourmet food, as we savored the unspoiled beauty of the escorting shorelines, the picturesque waters and the radiant glow of the setting sun.

Koala sighting in their natural habitat was scheduled for the next morning. These cute little creatures are essentially nocturnal animals and sighting them during the day, asleep on dense treetops, was as close as we could get to them. High up in the eucalyptus forests seemed to be their favorite haunt, providing them eucalyptus leaves for food and protection from predators.

We next headed to the Blue Mountains, a few hours west of Sydney. It is currently a major gateway to New South Wales, though once considered impassable. Of tourist interest in this area are the "Three Sisters Rocks"—a set of closely spaced steep rock pillars overlooking the Jamison Valley. Legend has it that three sisters of the Katoomba tribe fell in love with three brothers from the Nepean tribe. The tribal laws, however, sternly forbade the marriages. Fierce battles ensued and the three ladies were turned to stone for protection. But eventually the spell could not be reversed and they continue to remain in magnificent rock formation, towering nearly 3,000 feet into the skies.

A trip to Sydney is not considered complete without visiting the seaside suburb of Manly, an island seven miles from the city. A fifteen-minute ride on the Manly Jetcat Ferry brought us to this busy village with trendy cafes, art galleries and museums along the main promenade. Australia's national gemstone, the opal, was prominently displayed in varying colors in the jewelry stores—the black opal, the boulder opal, the white opal and the crystal opal, all polished and set in contemporary design. Women mulled around the showcases while the uneasy spouses awaited the damage to their wallets.

From Sydney, the motorcoach sped us to the airport for an hour-long flight to Melbourne. We were assigned to a quaint Victorian-style hotel with an ambience of grace from a bygone era. The bustling city displayed historic culture and old-fashioned charm from the narrowest alleys to the busiest promenades. Museums, shopping arcades, and landmark attractions lined the thoroughfares with a hint of old world ostentation. Sight-seeing included Fitzroy Gardens, the Parliament House and St. Patrick's Cathedral. The best of Melbourne was the Colonial Tramcar Restaurant on wheels—a vintage tram with velvet seats, burgundy carpets, fine cuisine and friendly service. We enjoyed gourmet meals on board while the tour guide updated us on the sights and sounds of this vibrant cultural capital. It was au revoir time again at the end of a fleeting two-day visit.

In continuation of what had been a very enjoyable vacation so far, the flight now took us across the Tasman Sea to neighboring New Zealand. Ferns and potted plants lined the walkways inside Auckland Airport. Palm trees and rocks added to the décor and the friendly New Zealanders contributed to a warm welcome to this "City of Sails." Checking into our hotel, I reminded the reception desk that we had requested an ocean-view room. The lady, seemingly amused, answered, "Madam, all rooms in this circular high-rise are bound to have an ocean view. The few inner rooms without a view might cost you more!" That shut me up for the rest of the trip. The entire day was one of leisure and individual exploring. This was a city abounding in beautiful beaches and bays, busy harbors and the matchless hospitality of the Aucklanders. The cabby drove us past landmarks and areas of historical significance to the Maoris. He assured us that walking tours were also an option, since streets here were safe because of strict gun control laws in place. For an American tourist that certainly was music to the ears!

The next couple of days were spent at a popular tourist resort on the Bay of Islands, located on the northernmost point of the North Island. The front desk setting was amidst natural rock-hewn caves from which miniature waterfalls leisurely trickled down to a lotus pond below. The quaint cottages nestling by the sand at the water's edge, the enclave of villas along bridled paths showcasing manicured landscaping and vistas of wild flowers, occasional fog rising in pockets, and the roaring rhythm of the sea made it a fresco of scenic beauty. On our drive along the ninety-mile beach, we saw the gigantic sand dunes co-existing in awesome harmony with the mighty ocean waves, displaying the time-honored pact of geography and geology. From Cape Reinga, the heavenly sighting of the meeting of the Tasman Sea and the Pacific Ocean and the cliff-style drop from the overview was enough to hold spectators rooted to their spots.

Our motor coach drive took us through the primordial rain forest amidst imposing, sky-high kaori trees. We enjoyed the tranquil atmosphere together with lessons in local history that was steeped in Maori culture. The Maoris are dark-haired, brown-skinned Polynesians who traced their ancestry back to a migration by canoes from Hawaii or Cook's Island around 1350. They were warrior people who brought with them ritualistic beliefs and farming techniques. Steeped in tradition these fascinating people are on a continuing mission of recognition in their homeland.

Exotic chirping birds of the forest played host when we stopped for a break for hot scones and cream, with a choice of tea or coffee. At Hobson's Beach where Captain Hobson had landed to initiate a negotiation with the Maoris, we saw the ancient hundred-foot war canoes used in their battles. Captain Hobson, governor of New Zealand, negotiated the Treaty of Waitangi with the Maori Chiefs, which granted England sovereignty over New Zealand in return for guarantees respecting their lands and possessions and rights as British subjects. The Maori temples with their unsightly carvings had withstood the ravages of time to become tourist attractions.

"A Hole in the Rock" cruise was an optional trip that we decided to take. It was located in the Pacific Ocean about sixty miles off the coast, but we did not quite foresee the pulsating, heart-throbbing, and intermittently spine-chilling nature of the ride! Ensuring that all passengers were firmly strapped to their seats, the high-speed catamaran initially cruised at reasonable pace around the Bay of Islands, highlighting sightings of whales, dolphins and seals. Past the Cape Brett lighthouse, without further announcements, it picked up speed and literally commenced to zoom through the "Hole in the Rock." Needless to say, the adrenaline in our systems started to zoom as well! It returned to cruise control minutes later, permitting us to breathe normally again. All of this makes for interesting reading in hindsight, but at the time kept us on the edge of our seats.

The two weeks of vacation were coming to an end. At the farewell banquet, we bade misty-eyed goodbyes to our trip mates, exchanged addresses and prepared for our flight back to the U.S. There was a bonus surprise en route—a two-day stopover at Fiji. Fiji Island was indeed paradise on earth showcasing the palm-fringed lagoons and the deep blue ocean which formed the backdrop of the lush tropical surroundings. On touchdown at the International Airport at Nadi, we were escorted to our hotel situated on a hill with picturesque views of the Sleeping Giant Mountain Ranges. While outdoor enthusiasts plunged into snorkeling, rafting through raging rapids and trekking in tropical rain forest, we chose to follow the less strenuous schedule of visiting the Bouma Falls, enduring bumpy rides on stone roads through sugarcane plantations on the outskirts of Nadi, visiting the Hindu temple and strolling through the Sleeping Giant Gardens that displayed over 500 varieties of orchids.

The next day at checkout time, we expressed annoyance at the lack of room television amenities in the so-called five star hotel. Much to our embarrassment we were told that Fiji did not have a TV station for them to render such service. Apparently they do have one now. An uneventful flight brought us back home after two fun-filled vacation weeks that went down in our journal of memoirs, hopefully to be followed by many more in the years ahead.

Eight

Greece and Cruise of the Mediterranean—July 1994

As the next year rolled in, so did our inner stirrings for travel. Having journeyed to distant lands that evoked the essence and character of the host countries, this time around we decided to seek a vacation package that covered both land and sea. Since this was going to be our first cruise, I read up relevant books and spent countless hours with the travel agent discussing outside stateroom accommodations, the experience of the nautical crew (we were not swimmers), the availability of licensed shipboard medical staff, and choice of cuisine for picky eaters. I was assured of the most gracious amenities afloat, unsurpassed service, cabins with plush interiors and panoramic views and even special theme dinners for vegetarians. The seasoned travel counselor, who had been very patient through all of the grilled questioning, finally set the icing on the cake by stating that exotic shopping at duty-free markets ashore would be the most irresistible feature of the cruise. That did it! We settled for travel to Greece followed by a cruise of the sun-painted islands on the Aegean and the Mediterranean Seas, sailing by night and exploring the islands by day. This trip seemed to offer camaraderie in conjunction with independence and more importantly, an easy-going pace that we had learned to value by now.

In July of 1994, we were part of the escorted tour

group flying into Athens, the fascinating capital of Greece and the seat of its ancient civilization. Once again, the day of arrival in this culturally affluent city was a day of leisure and independent exploration. We chose to relax in our hotel suite and familiarize ourselves with details of the archeological sites around Athens. History seemed to stand out amidst the ruins, majestically pronouncing its chequered past of glory and decline.

After a sumptuous breakfast bright and early next morning, we were in the motor coach driving to see first-hand the fabled ruins that still seemed to exude the pride of the civilization. Our first stop was at the Acropolis, meaning the "Sacred Rock." It rose sharply from the plains with sheltered caves and springs for relief. At the center of the Acropolis was the Parthenon, a temple dedicated to the Greek Goddess Athena. Its architecture and sculpture were a standing tribute to the enduring Greek art.

Ravaged by war and strife, some of the statues had found their way to the British Museum and the Louvre in Paris. Stepping out of the Acropolis, we walked a short distance to gaze at the ruins of the Theater of Dionysus—an open-air amphitheater that could seat an audience of several thousand people and had amazing acoustics that remain flawless to this day.

After a welcome stop for lunch we were on our way to the Temple of Poseidon in the mountain region of Cape Sounion. This imposing structure overlooking the sea was dedicated to Sea God Poseidon whose presence was considered inspirational and auspicious to all seafarers. It was the last sign of civilization the ancient Athenians saw as they sailed away from home and the first as they returned. Pillages and conquests resulted in the five-meter-high statue of Poseidon being destroyed beyond recognition, leaving only his foot for a souvenir. As evening turned to dusk, the tourist population converged here to watch the sun go down in all its glory—hues of yellow, red and orange vying with one another to dominate the sky. Our motor coach transported us back in good time to retire for the day. The next day we visited the archeological treasure at Delphi located on Mt. Parnassus, adjacent to the sanctuary of Apollo. The famous oracle of Delphi was believed to have originated in prehistoric times and exerted enormous influence on the Greek civilization. Following goat sacrifice, Pythia—the high priestess—would mount a tripod, breathing in the intoxicating smoke while entering a divine trance. The priests would then interpret the oracles of Pythia and relay the findings to the faithful seekers.

Back in our hotel room, we figured in the last-minute touches for the first cruise of our life, departing next morning. Keeping the anti-emetic tablets handy was top priority. We checked labels on baggages before setting them out for the ship's crew to pick up. We had already requested a wake-up call in the early hours, but paranoia got the better of us and we scrambled to the hallway to retrieve the suitcase carrying the alarm clock. But lo and behold—the baggages had all been picked up. Needless to say, after a disturbed night's sleep, bleary-eyed and tired, we boarded the ship and preferred to remain on sips of fluid till we were settled into the modality of life on board. Pampering by the shipboard crew helped placate some of the initial anxiety. The cabin was indeed furnished as projected and opened on to a private deck with a panoramic ocean view. "There was really no need to be so anxious," I told my husband. But I had spoken too soon. Just about then, the ship's public address system announced a mandatory life jacket drill with emergency sirens blaring in the background. To first-time oceanic passengers like us, this sounded more a foreboding of bad omen. With an unspoken sense of quiet panic, we joined the line of passengers headed to the drill arena. We were advised on the use of the life jackets, educated on the ship's escape routes and use of emergency lifeboats and finally wished a pleasant voyage, all in the same breath. I wondered if these cruises were going to end up being as much of an enigma as real life was!

Mykonos, a quintessential island in the Aegean Sea, was our first port of call. Gingerly stepping across the swaying gangway, we set foot on this picturesque island to stroll the streets that were lined with whitewashed houses and blue domed churches. I overheard someone say that Mykonos was a haven for connoisseurs of gold jewelry, and that they were headed that way. In minutes I was sprinting behind them with my disgruntled husband trying to keep pace. We surely could not depart from Greece without a gold souvenir! Later as we walked down the cobblestone alleys of this popular resort of the rich and the famous, we learned that the island was named after Apollo's grandson Mykons and that it was home to sea pirates till the beginning of the 19th century. A part of the town was a labyrinth of narrow streets probably designed to keep out the fierce winds and the ruthless buccaneers.

Petros the pelican, was the island's celebrated white feathered icon that chose to reside by the waterfront and grant audience to its indulgent fans. Carrying pleasant memories of this beautiful island and savoring the view of the Aegean sunset, we departed for overnight sailing to the island of Kusadasi in Turkey.

Kusadasi: We were anchored at this Turkish resort before daybreak, and set out to explore the island with a local tour guide. "Kusadasi" essentially meant Bird Island since birds frequented the area during seasonal migration. Driving past the green countryside we reached Ephessus, the best-preserved classical city in the Mediterranean. On foot hereon, we saw the ruins of the Temple of Diana and continued on past the ruins of the Library of Celsus, the thermal baths of Scolastika, the Roman stadium and the marketplace of Angora. We walked along the Arcadian Way which according to history had the distinct honor of hosting Mark Anthony and Cleopatra in procession. Back in the ship, we were informed by the captain that the next day would be a day of leisure since we would be cruising the Crete Sea and the Corinth Canal.

The day at sea was infinitely more relaxed than waking up to pre-determined schedules each morning. It was a "Greek to Me" day when the passengers were treated to Greek cuisines, and an evening of Greek dancing, singing and breaking of plates! During the day, we were encouraged to band together in groups and participate in the preparation of delicacies like "moussaka" (eggplant casserole), "spanakopita" (spinach pie), the popular dessert "baklava" and "tzatziki" (cucumber and yogurt sauce). Evening on the dance floor was the first of its kind that we had ever witnessed. The ship's crew in colorful costumes formed a circle linked by holding shoulders. Starting with the right foot and moving counter-clockwise, they danced slowly and gracefully to the rhythm of Greek music. The tempo soon started to rise, with the ship's guests joining in one by one. Before long it was a frenzied gyration, with music getting louder, and participants living it up by smashing ceramic plates on the ground to the cry of "Opah." We were content to watch the merrymaking from the sidelines. However, before long the steward herded all of us seated spectators into the dance circle. In the spirit of sportsmanship, everyone was expected to join in, he said. Before long we were dancing the night away, my sari probably contributing added color to the already colorful crowd. The ritual of plate shattering as a mode of celebration intrigued me more than ever. Nobody seemed to know why it was done, although some paused to consider it a legitimate question. Plate smashing continued unabated. The expression "opah," I was told, had no specific meaning—just living it up. At the end of an entertaining day, exotic food, and aching limbs, we were back in our cabin for the much-needed rest.

The ship resumed sailing overnight, bringing us to Itea by sunrise. A motor coach drove us to Meteora to see one of the most awe-inspiring sights in all of Greece—the Hanging Monasteries. They were perched on top of enormous rocks towering into the sky. Sculpted by Nature, these massive pinnacles rose from the plains of Kalampaka. The tour guide educated us on the history of this spectacle. As far back as the 10th century, hermits were believed to have climbed up here seeking solitude. Those of us that intended to negotiate the 200 rock-cut steps into the Varlaam Monastery were advised to observe the strict dress codes of long skirts or pants, covered arms and scarves covering the head. Appropriate outfits were available for tourists at the entrance to the monastery. Climbing those dizzy heights reminded me of the Sydney Bridge in Australia, but here the gratification was meant to be more spiritual than scenic. A glimpse into the monastic life deep within the caves of these rocks, clearly spelt self-inflicted solitude. There was contentment in their life style that was bereft of light or fresh air, sustenance on produce from adjacent clearings in the rocks, and knowledge of a final resting place within the rocks' crevices and fissures. Enlightening us on the historical front, the tour guide told us that in ancient times there were no rock-cut stairways to access these monasteries. Humans or essential goods were hauled up in net baskets using hand cranked rope pulleys. With obvious concern I asked the guide, "How often did they change the rope?" And he answered with a wry smile, "When the earlier one broke in action!" The insides of me started prompting an immediate downward trek. After a hurried viewing of the turrets carved around the terraced rock, we were back on the open patio, which permitted the luxury of light and air. Waving a hurried "au revoir" to the other distant monasteries perched at similar dizzy heights we sprinted down to level ground as fast as possible. We had set eyes on an amazing marvel of nature no doubt, but I personally was very content storing it in memory rather than ever wanting to repeat the experience. The motor coach brought us back to the ship and the sight of the swinging gangway over the choppy waters did not unnerve me as much anymore. We were past the freshman years in the world of travel.

The next morning we reached Portofino—the hub of celebrities with their private yachts. As we walked through this quaint town, a sense of relaxation seemed to descend on us although tourists here shared common ground with intellectuals and nobility. The Dolce Vita however stood apart as an exclusive arena where the celebrities and international elites chose to socialize, and commoners could steal a glimpse if their stars favored it.

Cruising on Italian waters, we reached the Isle of Capri off the Sorrentine peninsula. This lush, gorgeous island came alive with a beauty all its own. It probably ex-

ἱερὰ μονὴ
βαρλαὰμ
μετεώρων

№ 43529

Τιμὴ Εἰσόδυ
Σκευοφυλακίυ
Δρχ. 300

Hanging Monastery at Meteora

plained why many writers and scholars used Capri as the
inspirational setting for their works of literature. Anna
Capri, a sister township, was home to celebrity-chasing
paparazzi and the beautiful Villa San Michele Museum.
No tourist to this area ever misses a visit to the Blue
Grotto to enjoy an ethereal beauty that defies human
imagination. It is one of the world's most beautiful lime-
stone caves, with its name stemming from the blue light
that illuminates the inside of the cave picking up the reflection from the Mediterranean waters in which it is located. Only tiny rowing boats could negotiate the narrow
entrance to the cave and its low ceiling. Tourists were
asked to crouch to the floor of the gondola while the boatman attempted to row in, assuming the seas were calm

and there was bright sunshine overhead. If there ever were to be a mascot in nature's domain of unparalleled beauty, this would be it.

The next and last port of call on this cruise was Monte Carlo, the playground of the rich and the famous located in the tiny principality of Monaco. It is known for its casinos, its glamor and propensity for celebrity sighting. The ruling Prince Rainier acquired for it the exclusive status it now enjoys—the smallest but most prosperous of countries in the world. A couple of days in Monte Carlo were adequate to give us the ritzy feel—most cabs were the luxury models of BMWs and Mercedes, there were no visible shanty towns, and the hotels were furnished to make every occupant feel like royalty. However, a dizzy drop to reality set in at high-end restaurants. We could have entertained a family of four at Waldorf Astoria in New York for the price of gourmet cuisine for two in Monaco. Our local tour guide informed us that there were no issues of illegal immigration in Monaco, neither were there crimes or major social problems. In order to become a legal resident of the principality, one had to be fabulously rich—an obviously foregone conclusion. The Royal Palace and the castle style casinos were top tourists attractions in Monte Carlo as also the hillside crash site of Princess Grace Kelly. The 19th century Monaco Cathedral, which was her final resting place, was also slated for tourists to visit.

From Monaco we headed to Cannes, a resort town in the South of France where the world's most prestigious film festivals are held. Opened in 1870, it shot into fame as a fashionable hangout on the French Riviera. We could not afford anything more than a candid camera shot at the entrance of the ritzy hotel here.

Our final destination was Nice from where we were to board our flight back to the U.S. A must see for tourists in Nice is the Cours Saleya Flower Market which sported sidewalk cafes that served delightful pastries, and stands that were packed with ripe produce and fresh flowers in myriad hues. A never ending sea of humanity frequented this place all day long. Following a quick visit to the Russian Cathedral, the Matisse Museum that displayed innovative art, and the Parfumerie Fragonard where perfumes could be mixed and matched to the whims of the customer, we departed by motor coach for an hour-long ride to St. Paul de Vence, a beautiful medieval village with fortress walls surrounding the outskirts. This township is truly an art-lovers haven. Its winding, narrow cobblestone pathways laid in floral designs were lined with aging vine-covered stonewalls. Fountains and statues beckoned attention from their nooks in the walls. The art galleries at every street corner abounded in original artwork and Provencal crafts. There was a particularly stunning piece of pressed flowers on tea-rose-colored parchment paper and I could not resist acquiring it before leaving Provence. My husband demurely went along since it wasn't beyond our budget and this was to be the last of the purchases on this trip. We returned to Nice in time for our flight back to the U.S., although in our hearts we were loath to leave. All good things come to an end and so did this trip.

Nine

Far East: Thailand, Bali, Singapore and Hong Kong—October 1995

In the fall of 1995 we decided on a vacation to the Far East, to experience the balmy breeze of the tropics and relax amidst verdant coconut palms, indigenous fauna and exotic island fruits. Witnessing the vibrant cultural legacies of the land would be an added privilege. The framework of the two-week escorted trip would cover Bangkok, the resort island of Bali, Singapore and Hong Kong. We looked forward to sharing tales of jet setting adventures and insider perspectives with our like-minded fellow travelers and peers.

Our trans-Pacific airline flew us into Bangkok, Thailand's lively capital. We were driven to a luxury riverfront hotel, which would be our home for the next few days. The thematic hotel décor revolved around the Orchid. There were orchids in varying hues at the entrance, inviting orchid arrangements in the foyer, orchids in gleaming brass pots along the hallways and more orchids in the suites. The view from our balcony of the historic Chao Phraya River—the "River of Kings"—was awesome as was the shimmering backdrop of Bangkok's skyline by night. As always, the day of arrival was invariably a day of rest and it was no different in Bangkok. A short walk through the neighborhood reflected the general friendliness of the people and the diversities of the country's colors and flavors.

The next morning, we set out by motor coach on a city tour arriving at Bangkok's Grand Palace, the symbol of Thailand's monarchy. Built by King Rama, the first ruler of the Chakri dynasty, it stood on enormous grounds with the exquisite buildings in Siamese architecture housing royal residences, audience halls, pavilions, and the gilded royal chapel Wat Phra Kaew—home of the legendary Emerald Buddha. Pinnacles of the palaces were capped in solid gold. We gazed in amazement at the towering spires with gateways guarded by figures of mythological monsters, the Dusit Maha Prasat audience hall where there was a throne in mother-of-pearl that could seat only a duly crowned king, and the Royal Pantheon displaying statues of past sovereigns in exclusive works of art. It was interesting to know that this Palace was the setting for the Broadway musical *The King and I*.

On the northern end of the palace was the chapel housing the Emerald Buddha. It is considered the most sacred statue in all of Thailand and held in national veneration and esteem. Carved entirely from a single piece of jade, this thirty-inch statue was discovered accidentally in 1434 when a bolt of lightning hit a pagoda, crumbling the plaster to reveal the wonder beneath. Worshippers are required to be appropriately attired before entering this exotic Buddhist temple to which numerous miracles are attributed.

After a short break for a light lunch, we headed to the city's many ornate temples that manifest Thailand's Buddhist heritage. The Temple of the Golden Buddha (Wat Traimit) is the repository of the world's largest gold statue of Buddha, gracefully seated with legs crossed in a posture of penance. Ten feet high and weighing over five tons, this imposing statue is believed to radiate an inner divinity to the faithful.

The Temple of the Reclining Buddha (Wat Pho) was unique in its presentation. Here the magnificent gold-covered statue was 150 feet long and fifty feet high. In a reclining posture with feet and eyes carved in mother-of-pearl, it was designed to imply the passing of Buddha into Nirvana, the ultimate salvation.

On our drive back to the hotel, we saw Buddhist temples and statues in varying sizes and shapes, quaint rock gardens, bell towers, and fortunetellers at street corners. This was indeed a country of the exotic East which abounded in spectacular temples and enduring Buddhist traditions, and the tranquil rivers and lusciously green hillsides added to its ambivalent charm. I did notice that most homes here—affluent and otherwise—had a miniature temple-like structure at the entrances. The tour guide explained to us that in Thailand, people believe that ancestral and natural spirits inhabit every parcel of land and that before a house is constructed, a dwelling place called San Phra Poom should be provided for the head-spirit known as "Chaotee." It is in layman's language, a "spirit house" set at eye level. An offering to the "chaotee" is believed to render protection from evil spirits and help maintain good luck in days to come. A delectable Thai dinner at the hotel was awaiting us on our return. We headed to the banquet hall which was done up tastefully in an eclectic combination of contemporary and old-world charm. Pretty and petite Thai girls in traditional costumes welcomed us with "Wai"—a Thai greeting with folded hands and bowed heads similar to the Indian "namaste." Thai hot and sour soup was served for starters, followed by cabbage salad, rice and massaman curry. Mango ice cream was the dessert for the evening. The dinner was capped off with Thai iced tea, creamy and sweetened, which reminded me of a welcome version of Indian "chai."

The next day's itinerary listed a packed schedule with visits to the Rose Garden and the Floating Market in the rural Ratchaburi Province, seventy miles outside Bangkok. A half hour's drive brought us to the Rose Garden, situated on seventy-five acres of manicured grounds around a lake. Elephant shows, Thai boxing sword fighting, and ongoing cultural programs were some of the highlights here. We opted for a Thai lunch-cultural show combo, which catered to our appetites and embellished our aesthetic horizons. Following this was the hour-long ride along fertile rice fields to the Damnoen Saduak Floating Market. The tour guide utilized the ride to introduce the uninitiated tourists to the Thai elemental connection with Buddhism and its generational adherence to age-old beliefs. Thailand, he said, was a predominantly Buddhist nation whose culture, tradition and way of life have been preserved through daily practices and performances. Theravada Buddhism (Teaching of the Elders) is believed to be the oldest form of Buddhism prevalent in Thailand. It emphasized the humanity of Buddha, his path to Enlightenment and final attainment of Nirvana. The teachings stress self-reliance and following the path of the Great Master.

The Mahayana and Tantrayana forms of Buddhism, we were told, highlighted the supernatural attributes of Buddha and his ability to guide the faithful to Enlightenment. Buddhism was believed to have originated out of dissatisfaction of ritualistic Hindu practices. It categorically rejected the "caste system" but retained the role of Karma (one's deeds) in repeated rebirths. Buddhist values were apparently inculcated in young adults by having them spend quality time in a monastery in monk's robes and shaven heads, presumably the rite of passage that every man was supposed to undergo.

At the conclusion of the question and answer session in the motor coach, we had reached the outskirts of our destination. It was rural, unspoiled and yet inviting. At the jetty, we boarded long-tailed boats in groups and were ferried through small canals to arrive at the famous Floating Market. Hundreds of Thai vendors sporting traditional straw hats paddled their boats up and down, laden with fresh fruits, vegetables and steaming hot delicacies. It was interesting to watch boat to boat trading as well as boat to shore transactions. The Floating Market unmistakably represented yesteryears of Thailand when waterways were the medium for conducting business.

Elephants continue to play an important role in Thai society. The following morning was a dedicated excursion to a local elephant camp. Elephant rides were meant to be the highlight of the visit and most of our trip mates seemed to enjoy the proximity to the tamed pachyderms. When time came for us to mount the elephants from raised platforms with the mahouts in attendance, my husband quickly whisked me away from the site to the far end of the camp.

"There is no way I am going to let you go on that elephant ride," he said.

I didn't get it. "What's the point of coming here then? It's bound to be such a thrilling experience," I replied.

"Just imagine if you fell from that height," he said. "It would either be fatal or end up being in a vegetative state. Is that your idea of thrill?"

I now realized that the emergency physician in him had started to work overtime. I was never going to be allowed an elephant or camel ride as long as I lived! We walked back to the motor coach and bided time till our trip mates returned for the drive back to the hotel. The afternoon was allotted for leisure, and I decided to indulge in Thai massage in our hotel room while my husband set out to explore the neighborhood on foot.

At the appointed hour, four uniformed ladies arrived equipped with a bamboo mat, a table that resembled a mammogram biopsy gurney and a few frosted glass containers with relaxants. They gave me a choice between the mat and the gurney. I didn't settle for either and insisted that they give me the massage on my bed. Reluctantly they agreed, and the four of them removed the sheets and replaced them with the mat. With the minimal clothing I was allowed, they got me positioned on the mat and in perfect unison all four jumped onto the four corners of the bed and commenced working on me. Each of them took charge of a limb and the two by my head worked on my shoulders and forehead as well. They babbled nonstop about the techniques to relieve muscle-ache, encourage blood flow in the system, infuse energy, and work on pressure points. In less than half an hour I was one sore mass from head to foot, enduring all their stretches and manipulations. A brief respite came in the form of skin care when they worked on my face with a sort of scrub made from tamarind fruit to exfoliate and purify the skin. And then they were back again fixing stress-knots in the muscle and bending my limbs to yoga-like postures, draining in the process what little energy I had left. The vigorous and forceful rubbing of the head and neck had me feeling pretty faint and I wondered if I was headed for an out-of-body experience. At the end of the hour they departed, leaving a prone and fatigued body to relish the aftermath of professional workmanship. Soon thereafter, my husband returned and seeing my condition started to check me out for paralysis. In the next couple of hours though, I was able to hobble around the room hoping to return to normalcy by daybreak. So much for the hyped ethnic massage.

Our last day in Bangkok concluded with the popular boat ride on the Chao Phraya River. It offered us an unseen side of the Thai rural heartland as we sailed past wooden houses on stilts and banana plantations lining the waterway for miles on end. Homes on the riverfront ranged from affluent mansions to tin-roof shacks. Ambulance boats plied on the waters transporting patients to hospitals on land. This was the first of such services that we had ever witnessed. The boatman devoutly pointed to the Wat Arun—the Temple of Dawn—another of the many venerated Buddhist temples along the waterway. We had just about reached the pier when the dark clouds overhead descended in a thunderous downpour, drenching us to the skin.

The next morning a local airline flew us into Dempasar in the resort island of Bali. Immigration lines at the airport were long and the high humid temperatures had us soaking in perspiration. When my turn came, I presented my passport to the immigration officer little realizing what was about to occur in the next few minutes. The officer reviewed the passport briefly and then looked up at me and back at my passport, intently flipping through the pages from cover to cover. He then asked me for my name and address in the United States. Even as I replied, I felt an odd sense that something was amiss. The officer told me to step out of line and stand aside. My husband, who was right behind me, now moved up to the desk to present his passport and find out what exactly was going on. The officer took one quick look at his passport, confirmed his last name and asked him to step aside as well. We both were then marched under police escort to a nearby room, the door bolted and we were seated on a wooden bench while uniformed officials checked out our credentials on the computer.

It was a nightmare of nightmares not knowing why we were there in the first place or what had caused us to be the apparent suspects that we were made out to be. No Miranda rights were read to us. A few heads converged around the computer while a few others discussed the findings in hushed tones. In my own head, a barrage of questions was kicking in as we waited out the process. Did we have the right to remain silent, did we have the right to an attorney in this distant land, and more importantly, could any of our answers be used against us in their court of law? It was a good half hour before a wry-looking senior official came up to us and said that we were now free to leave. I do not know whether relief or anger prevailed at that point. I thanked the officer for their decision but also informed him in no uncertain terms that we were not about to budge an inch unless we were told what caused us to be brought to that room in such an abrupt manner. The officer paused, got his thoughts together and replied, "Madam, your last name, hometown and country matched that of a drug dealer that we were looking for. We have been trying to nab him for months." I gasped. "Officer," I said, "it's a 'he' that you are looking for and I am a 'she'—a very basic gender difference." He nodded in agreement, no further words were spoken and we were ushered out of that room to our waiting motor coach. Our peers couldn't wait to hear the details. The entire group was in a state of shock over the incident. From then on, we decided to look over our shoulders and watch out for each other for the rest of the trip. Thus began our sojourn in this coveted resort island, the great unknown that was Bali.

Our hotel here with its own private beach was the epitome of luxury, set amidst groves of bamboo palms overlooking a manmade lake. The front desk had for a backdrop, gorgeous Balinese sculptures gilded in shining gold and the gardens welcomed their visitors with Balinese effigies. At a vantage location on the grounds was the statue of Lord Ganesha—the Elephant God—sitting under a thatched roof with tall grass and waterfalls enhancing the ambience. Breakfast in this resort hotel was unique and heavenly. Relaxing in the lounge and watching the frothy waves of the turquoise ocean wash up on the white sandy beach we feasted on a spread of Indonesian, Thai, Japanese, Chinese, Indian, and Western cuisine. The display of exotic and mouth-watering island fruits accounted for the long lines in that direction. This island of the Gods was indeed a living legend, displaying Nature's bounty and a culture based on harmony among mankind. The dictates of divinity were omnipresent. Stepping back in time as it were, one cannot but admire the Balinese grace so interspersed with tradition and rituals. Balinese celebration of life centered around devotion to the Gods and rituals from the Hindu religion, endorsing them as feasts for the immortal soul.

Since most part of our stay in Bali was meant to be spent at leisure, we explored the island on foot—the land that Balinese consider to be a spiritual inheritance. Strolling along the beach in the early morning hours, we were privy to sightings of saronged fishermen preparing to cast their nets in the ocean. We walked past terraced, fertile paddy fields, coconut palms, mango groves, and acacia trees as we approached the nearby village. The local temple grounds seemed to sit amidst sprawling banyan trees while fragrances of jasmine and magnolia wafted past us. Hibiscus, bougainvilleas and orchids lined the roadsides. Kingfishers, egrets, and cuckoos flew past with an agenda of their own while occasional monkeys walked alongside to check us out. The village seemed strangely quiet as wise-looking elders squatted in their front yards, soaking up the morning sun.

At dinnertime we were entertained by Balinese dancers dressed in richly woven, shimmering sarong outfits and headgears of fresh flowers. The morrow marked the last day of our stay on the island. While part of me looked forward to departing at the earliest in view of our horrendous experience at the airport here, the other part of me was reluctant to bid adieu to this veritable paradise on earth. A guided tour took us to the 13th century Kehen Temple in the mountainous region of Bangli. It is one of the largest Hindu temples in Bali and uniquely carved in Hindu and Polynesian styles. This particular temple had three courtyards, each to be entered through a towering gateway. The middle courtyard abounded in banyan trees for purposes of veneration, we were told. We then headed to Kintamani for a view of the dormant Mt. Batur, a double volcano with the huge outer rim rising a mile high.

We spent the evening carefully packing and securing our baggage, making sure that nobody could access it to throw in a packet of marijuana or other contraband items. The gallows would of course be imminent in that case! The following day saw us on a two-hour flight to Singapore, the Garden City of the East. Our elegant high-rise hotel here commanded a gorgeous view of the imposing skyline of the city. The Singapore harbor and backwaters as seen from our balcony was more like Van Gogh beckoning nature on canvas. Singapore is an island state at the southern tip of the Malayan Peninsula, a captivating destination that presented an eclectic blend of ethnicities but retaining alongside their own distinct heritages. Built in the 1880s, the then Fort Siloso served as the last bastion of the British forces during the Japanese invasion of Singapore. The city is one of the cleanest known and the population consisting of Chinese, Malays, Hindus and Moslems live in commendable harmony. Malay, English, Mandarin and Tamil are the official languages.

The first of our two-day stay here was spent visiting locales of tourist interest. The towering Raffles Hotel, we were told, is referred to as the "Grande Dame of Singapore." Built in 1887, it has maintained its inimitable grandeur with periodic structural relief. Brilliant sunrays shone on the cylindrical high-rise, further accentuating the charm and grace of this icon. It stands to reason that this 19th century hotel had been a hideaway for many celebrities like Somerset Maugham, Rudyard Kipling and Charlie Chaplin. As we drove past the busy Singapore harbor, we could not help but notice the gigantic cranes for miles on end, silhouetted against the clear blue skies. Singapore, to this day, is one of the world's busiest ports conducting maritime trade. The Central Business District—home to banks and financial institutions—was an astounding study in state-of-the-art high-rises displaying marvels of steel in partnership with glass. We then headed to Chinatown for a view of the Buddha Tooth Relic Temple, housing the sacred tooth of Buddha in a pillar of gold. Our last stop for the day was the Mariamman Temple also situated in Chinatown. Built in 1827, its humble beginnings were in wood and thatched modem and several subsequent renovations have brought it to its present impressive state. Dedicated to Goddess Mariamman who is worshipped for health and prosperity, the main entrance to the temple is through a tower called "Gopuram" which carried six tiers of sculptured deities. Visible from afar, it caters to devotees who wish to pray without actually entering the temple precincts.

We set out next morning by motor coach to the cable car station from where we boarded the cable car to Sentosa Island—home to historical enclaves, theme parks, underwater world and a lost civilization. Sentosa, meaning "peace and tranquility," was formerly a fishing village turned British military base. Merlion Park, the island state's icon, revolves around a 28-ft.-high lion head with a fish body resting on a crest of waves built in cement fondue. History goes that the head is representative of a lion believed to be spotted by Prince Utama when he discovered Singapore in 11 A.D. The fish tail symbolizes the ancient city of Temasek, meaning "sea" in Javanese, translating to Singapore's humble beginnings as a fishing village.

The appearance of the Lost Civilization City transported us back in time to a silent history that embodied hieroglyphic gateways, mythological motifs and ancient carvings of lions. A trip into volcano land was meant for those who sought adventure. It transported willing tourists on a simulated subterranean journey into the center of the earth to supposedly trace the evolution of life. It involved sitting in a pit cage and riding down to the earth's belly which sizzled with fire. The journey back was a catapulted return hurtling through tremors and hot air. We quickly excused ourselves when we heard the tour guide say that Professor Hugo in 1911 undertook this challenge and disappeared without a trace! Later in the day, we strolled through the Fountain Gardens amidst the musical sounds of flowing water and getting to see first-hand the three dancing fountains in spiral formation. It helped soothe our frayed nerves from the Hugo story. At sundown, we headed back to our hotel to prepare for our flight to Hong Kong next morning. The harrowing experience at Bali's Dempasar Airport was still vivid in our minds and we fervently hoped and prayed that there should be no similar enactment for the remainder of our trip. Arrival and airport clearance at Hong Kong was uneventful.

We were assisted to our hotel, which commanded a glamorous view of the bay and the towering skyscrapers of Hong Kong. This metropolis undoubtedly stands out as one of Asia's sophisticated destinations that brings alive the fusion of the West and the East. The dazzle of modern life here in conjunction with reverence for ancient traditions helps maintain a balanced culture. Ancient Chinese temples with smoldering incense within exist alongside state of the art buildings that house billion dollar ventures.

Our sight-seeing commenced with a funicular rail ride to Victoria peak where many of the rich and famous reside. Bamboo trees, dwarf pines and hibiscus dotted the hillsides. From the peak, we got a panoramic view of one of the busiest waterways in the world—the South China Sea stretching for miles beyond the mainland to Macao. After a steep descent back, we headed to Repulse Bay, in the southern part of Hong Kong Island. We were told that this beachgoer's haven was at one time a stronghold for pirates. Two large colorful statues currently dominate the scene—one of Goddess Kwun Yum (Goddess of Mercy) and the other of Goddess Tin Hau (Goddess of the Sea). Leaving Repulse Bay, we boarded a traditional Chinese sampan boat with wooden seats and a roof overhead for a ride to Aberdeen Fishing Village to get a peek into the lives of the fisher folks. Brightly colored trawlers served as their floating homes. People spent their entire lives on these boats with family and pets. Pungent-smelling salted fish were set out to dry on the roofs of these boats. Fish being their staple food, it's possible that they had learned to live with the odor. We then sailed past the multi-decked Jumbo Floating Restaurant, the size of a cruise ship and believed to be the largest of its kind in the world. It was ornately decorated with rows of colorful lights and gilded dragons. Delectable Cantonese cuisine was believed to be the hallmark of this fine dining establishment.

Early next morning, we were on the road again driving past colorful street markets and serene temples. On the streets, lion and dragon dancers performed to celebrate an auspicious event. Lion dancers apparently are believed to bring good luck since a lion spirit has an important place in Chinese mythology. The sights and sounds around dispelled the notion that Hong Kong is all skyscrapers and world-class shopping malls. Rich traditions and Chinese culture unequivocally existed alongside. At lunchtime, we were treated to a "Dum Sum" (meaning touch your heart) cuisine consisting of varieties of dumplings and steamed dishes. Honeyed banana fritters were served for dessert followed by "Yum Cha" (tea drinking)—a twelve-hundred-year-old tradition in Chinese culture. After my concerted efforts at sign language to learn why their teapots were so small, I gleaned from the waitress that smaller the teapot, better the fragrance. A cup of tea always made a strong presence in Hong Kong's culinary world. We resumed our motor coach ride for a view of the world's longest road and rail suspension bridge—the Tsing Ma Bridge—while the guide lectured us on the ancient art of Feng Shui. He was obviously speaking in English, but I had to fine-tune my faculties to be able to jot down comprehensible notes. He went on to say that they believe that Feng Shui elements of wind and water generated prosperity and vibrancy of this international city.

Our presence in Hong Kong in the month of October gave us the unique privilege of witnessing their traditional welcome of the "Harvest Moon" with special lantern carnivals. A colorful fire-dragon procession originating near Causeway Bay, displayed a 200-foot-long fiery dragon made up of hundreds of burning joss sticks. The "Symphony of Lights" is probably the world's largest light and sound show, covering a vast expanse of buildings along the Victoria Harbor. It presented an unforgettable spectacle of colored lights and laser beams, synchronized to music and narration. The show is believed to depict the pervading diversity and spirit of Hong Kong.

Proceeding to the Kowloon District, we stopped at the Chi Lin Nunning which to this day maintains the Tang monastic lifestyle, sporting Buddhist halls and Zen-style rock gardens. We also saw the world's largest seated outdoor Buddha—a serene 8-feet-high bronze statue on Lantau Island. Following this was a trip to the Jade Market for souvenirs. I did not dare venture into much shopping here for fear of repercussions at the Customs in the U.S., especially since I had put together a fairly sizable collection so far.

The next day was an assigned day of leisure before we headed back home. My husband and I decided to use the time visiting Macao—a tiny jewel-like enclave on

South China Sea, forty miles from Hong Kong. Disembarking at the jetfoil terminal after a fifteen-minute hovercraft ride, we set out to explore the island on foot. Macao is home to a colorful mix of races—Chinese, Portuguese, Dutch, Spanish and British. Walking down cobblestone streets, past the pealing church bells and apothecaries at street corners, we reached a building that had the contemporary look of a Mall. Clothing, shoes, leather goods and even gold jewelry were available here at a fraction of Hong Kong prices, presumably because they were manufactured on the island.

We walked past the ruins of St. Paul's Church built by Jesuits in the 17th century, and visited the Kun Iam Temple, built in the 14th century. Back in our hotel, we congregated at dinnertime to bid farewell to each other and to the beautiful city of Hong Kong. An eventful flight and a smooth walk through Customs concluded this trip.

Ten

The Danube River Cruise: Hungary, Slovakia, Germany, Austria and Czech Republic—August 1996

Our travels had, by now, become high points in our lives and fostered in us a recurring passion to see the world's alluring destinations. Having enjoyed sailing the high seas once before, the lure of a cruise surfaced again. I was told that river cruises could be as diverse as they were magnificent. We opted for the Danube River Cruise, which promised to be a true riverboat experience with a European ambience. The ship was to chart a course along the Danube River covering Hungary, Slovakia, Germany, Austria and the Czech Republic. Classic waterways, medieval history beckoning from the shores, limitless horizons, and waking up to new destinations were some of the compelling features of this cruise.

Flying into Vienna in early August from an eastern gateway city in the U.S., we were transferred forthwith to a riverboat with a passenger capacity of 150. Although much smaller and less luxurious than the ocean liners, this little ship offered us the warmth and welcome of an extended family. A cup of coffee on the sun deck seemed ideal while watching the changing vistas of sea and sky. We felt a new level of indulgence as the ship's crew made every effort to speak comprehensible English when pampering us with shipboard services. We congregated for an early dinner with the captain and his crew. While we relished the ethnic culinary meal—the main course being the Hungarian Goulash (a stew of meat, potatoes, onions and paprika)—the captain educated us on the history of the Danube River. It is believed to have originated at the confluence of the Breg and Brigach in the Federal Republic of Germany and wound its way into Austria where all waltzes have sung the praises of the Blue Danube. From there on, it flowed past the southern foothills of erstwhile Czechoslovakia into Hungary right through the bustling capital of Budapest.

Continuing on a more sluggish note, the Danube glides past Bulgaria, covering 700 miles through Romania before spilling into the Black Sea. Fabled in legend and song as the "river of rivers," a journey along the Danube was a journey through the splendors of Europe's past and the fascinating diversity of the present. In order to help us savor the beauty and medieval history of the area, the ports of call, the captain said, would be Budapest and the picturesque towns of Szentendre, Visegrad and Estergom along the Danube Bend, Bratislava in modern Slovakia, Passau in Germany and Vienna in Austria. The cruise was to terminate in Vienna and following a two day stay there, we would be flying into Prague, the stunning capital of the Czech Republic before heading back to the U.S.

Back to our riverboat cruise, an overnight sailing brought us to Budapest in Hungary—a land-locked nation filled with old-world charm, castles and folklore. The entire day was dedicated to a tour of this capital city which is basically a union of two cities situated on opposite sides of the Danube River—the colorful hills of Buda and the wide boulevards of Pest. The cultural, political, and commercial pulses of the country appeared to throb in and around Budapest. We visited St. Stephen's Cathedral that towered in the backdrop, the Castle Hill housing St. Mathias Church and the National Gallery, the Citadelle on Gellert Hill where we saw the Hungarian Statue of Liberty of a woman holding up a palm leaf, and the monument-filled Heroes Square. On an optional tour, we were educated on Budapest's unique Jewish history and escorted to the largest synagogue in the world, known also as the Hungarian Holocaust Memorial. Deserving special mention is the little town of Kalocsa founded in the 11th century by the first Hungarian monarch King Stephen. It is not only the paprika capital of the world but also a center for spirited Hungarian horsemanship, where we witnessed whip-cracking cowboys perform with skill and daring.

With an operetta performance on board by Hungarian musicians and singers, our ship then sailed into the Danube Bend, which is the heartland of Hungary's history and one of the celebrated centers of the cultural life of the Hungarian Renaissance. The three picturesque towns that we briefly visited were Szentendre, Visegrad and Estergom. Szentendre, located twelve miles from Budapest, is essentially an artist town with musicians and mimes at every street corner. On display were some of the most beautiful pieces on love and motherhood by Hungary's greatest ceramist Magrit Kovacs.

Visegrad, on a horse-shoe bend of the Danube, sported the ruins of a mighty citadel atop a hill which was once a repository for crown jewels during the reign of the Renaissance monarch King Matthews. The castle of Visegrad, at first glance, looked as though its upper walls were extending up to the clouds and the lower bastions reaching down to the river. Estergom was dominated by its great Basilica, the largest church in Hungary built in 1856 and continues to remain as the seat of the Arch-bishop. Marble and mosaic prominently figured in this imposing cathedral, while the stunning collections of bejeweled objects were a feast for the eye. The dazzling centerpiece was the Corvinus—the Ceremonial Cross fashioned by goldsmiths in Paris, blending the Gothic and Renaissance styles. The Hungarian countryside looked inviting on the road to the picturesque Wachau Valley where we stopped for a drink in the wine town of Durnstein. Houses here were typically in rows, sandwiched between rocky hillsides. Adjoining the valley was the 900-year-old Melk Abbey handed to the Benedic-tine monks by the Babenburgs. The yellow monastery is a Baroque masterpiece perched on a cliff-top site overlook-ing the Danube. The imperial rooms of the medieval cas-tle are home to the abbey museum, which carried exhibits of "Melk Abbey in its Past and Present."

Back on the riverboat, we were headed to Slovakia, Europe's youngest country which gained independence in January 1993. Its pioneering residents were at the time striving to make their mark in the emerging new world. Bratislava, the present capital, also happened to be the Hungarian capital in the 16th century and had witnessed nineteen coronations including that of Queen Maria Theresa. It was home to the Celts, the Romans, the Ger-mans and Slavs. The rich inheritance of the past had left its imprint on the cuisine and lifestyle of the present day Slovakians. Most of the castles and churches constructed in Gothic, Renaissance and Baroque styles house muse-ums, public offices and seats of cultural legacy. Our final port of call on the cruise before disembarking at Vienna was Passau, a backwater town in a lost corner of Ger-many. This city sees the Danube flow out of Germany at the confluence of the three rivers Danube, Inn and Ilz. Outstanding among the many historical buildings and opulent abbeys in Passau, was the Cathedral of St. Stephen, which houses the largest church organ in the world. The sounds of the organ were phenomenal though to me the notes sounded appropriate for a funeral. I attribute it entirely to my own utter lack of ear for music. This little town presented a Mediterranean ambience since picturesque archways joined one house to the next. A visit to the Passau Glass Museum was a must to the souvenir collectors on the cruise. There were rare and exquisite glass objects on display—some centuries old and some finished minutes ago. We watched the craftsmen mold their glass creations in mouth-blown tradition, combining beauty and creativity. I could not walk out of this seemingly magical world without acquiring a souvenir—an affordable bright yellow vase topped off with delicate purple iris petals.

An overnight cruise brought us into Vienna, the capital city of Austria. After the usual disembarkation formalities, we were bused to a premier hotel in the heart of the city across from The Stadt Park, known to be one of Vienna's most beautiful grounds. Since the day of arrival in any city was deemed a day of rest, we spent the evening strolling through the park and enjoying Nature at its most artistically inspired. Ornamental shrubs and vistas of flowers vied with each other in lending grace and color to the many monuments and statues. Vienna undoubtedly is the musical capital of the world and its aura is seen and felt all around. We saw novices trying their hands at violin, older couples seated on benches along the garden paths sharing mouth-watering Viennese tortes and many others simply pausing by sculptures of the prodigies in focused admiration while enjoying music ensembles by budding aspirants. "If music be the food of love, play on" is a famous referred quote from Shakespeare's *Twelfth Night* and to this and here were dedicated maestros like Mozart, Beethoven and Strauss. Stepping onto the streets, we saw numerous coffee houses boasting the best in chestnut cream cakes, cherry strudels and lingonberry meringue tortes. Viennese pastry is possibly the only other consort to musical fame in the Austrian world.

In the morning a waiting motor coach took us on a city tour of Vienna. Our first stop was at St. Stephen's Square—the sprawling centerpiece of the city with its showcase cathedral that featured a Romanesque façade, Baroque altars and Gothic towers. Housing the Hapsburg crypt and the filigreed Pilgram pulpit, it is to this day the proud heritage of the Viennese people as also a mute witness to the turbulent history of this city during World War II. As we were driven along the Ringstrasse, a wide boulevard that circles the city, I could only marvel at the opulence we saw—lavish palaces, world class art museums, and medieval architecture that stood out as the city's hallmarks. The Austrian satirist Karl Kraus had rightly said, "The streets of Vienna are paved with culture, the streets of other cities with asphalt." Our next stop was the ornate and spectacular Schonbrunn Palace—a former residence of the powerful Hapsburg dynasty. Set on grounds that host the most meticulously planned gardens studded with bronze statues, bowers of roses, rows of perfectly trimmed yews, and flaming red geraniums, sections of this palatial structure remain open for operas and musical concerts. In the capital city's marketplace, we saw Vienna's unique Art Clock—a linear clock built in 1912 which plays music while showing "hourly sovereigns" from Austria's historical past.

The next day, we took a walking tour through the Hofburg grounds which host the impressive imperial palace of the Hapsburg dynasty. We later stopped at one of Vienna's famous cafés for a taste of "guglhuph"—the most delicious sponge cake served with coffee and brimming with "schlage" (cream).

In the evening, we opted for the musical Vienna at the famed Kursalon Concert Hall. This was a special concert featuring Vienna's renowned musical legacy.

The next morning was a half-day of leisure and the tour guide suggested a not so sensational venture for those interested in trying it out. It was a picnic to a graveyard—a 300,000-plot central cemetery where many celebrities including Strauss and Beethoven have been laid to rest amidst lush greenery and ornate headstones. Inspiration was everywhere in Vienna but the idea of a graveyard picnic did not inspire me.

Bidding goodbye to this soul-stirring city we boarded the flight to Prague, the historic capital of Czech Republic. The nation was re-emerging from Communism faster than we thought. We were assigned to one of the better hotels, and were pleasantly surprised at the many creative and upscale touches in the lobby. We were in for an even pleasanter surprise when we entered our room with the keycard. The TV screen was flashing a personalized welcome message, referring to us by our name and hometown in the U.S. It was the first time we had ever encountered a welcome in this fashion and I could not resist reaching out for my camcorder to record it. There was a visibly rapid transition to capitalism in Prague. Off to an early start the next morning, we were driven through the ageless bastions of astonishing architecture with spirals and castles that outlined the city. Prague was in itself, a study in ancient Gothic, Baroque, and Renaissance architecture, which remained untouched by natural disaster or war.

Our first stop was the Karlstejn Castle, which is situated on a mountaintop with turreted watch towers. The Czech kings were believed to have ruled from here and it currently houses the crown jewels of the Bohemian kingdom. Its grandeur has held its own in spite of the excesses of postwar redevelopment. Within the complex were located the St. Vitus Cathedral sporting towering Gothic spires and currently the seat of the Archbishop of Prague, the Romanesque Basilica of St. George, a monastery and manicured palace gardens. We then headed to one of the most visited sites in all of Prague—the magnificent St. Charles Bridge built in the 14th century across the Vltava River. Less than half a mile long, it stands on three Gothic bridge towers with Baroque styled statues of saints installed on either side. During the day, street musicians and souvenir stalls lined the bridge vying for tourist attention. Our tour guide advised us to hold off on crystal shopping till we got to Stare Mesto which would be our next stop. This was the old city that originated on the banks of Vltava, displaying much of Prague's best architecture, huge market squares and an array of crystal shopping centers. These stores carried everything in crystal from shimmering chandeliers to boxed stemware, from lampshades to five-foot-high vases and from glittering jewelry to Cinderella-style slippers. After purchasing a few boxed wine glasses, I had to pull myself away since space constraint in our suitcases was getting to be an issue.

Driving through the New City that surrounded the

Old City, we had a glimpse of the Opera House and the city museum, feeling as though the three cities were ensconced in one.

We wrapped up this tour in a very unconventional manner. A forty-mile motor coach ride took us to a 13th-century silver mining town called Kutna Hora. We first visited St. Barbara's Church there, and then walked down the street to another church the likes of which one might not normally encounter. It was the spine-chilling Kostnice or "Bone Church," which was lined entirely with human skulls and bones, right from the entrance up to the altar. Ghoulish as it may seem, the skulls and bones were fashioned into chandeliers and streamers, imposing pillars, pyramids, and coats of armor incorporating every size and shape of human bones. It was a chilling, macabre sight. The story goes that the town was ravaged by the plague of 1870 and unable to bury the thousands dead for want of space, so their bones and skulls were used in this fashion as a lasting memorial to them. Wood carver Frantisek Rint believed he brought in a decorative touch when he created these displays to adorn the church, its walls, the archways, and the altar. We were told that an estimated 40,000 human bones were used. As we walked out of this ossuary, I looked up and around one last time reminding myself that each and every skull and bone there did at some point belong to a living breathing human being. What a way to end a vacation, but then again it served as a grim reminder of the frailty of all mortal beings—committed from earth to earth, ashes to ashes, and dust to dust. Macbeth's famous words in Shakespeare's play came to mind:

Chandelier of human skulls and bones in Kutna Hora

Life's but a walking shadow, a poor player
That struts and frets his hour upon the stage
And then is heard no more.

We departed on a more sober note this time around and boarded our flight home.

Eleven

The Scandinavian Odyssey: Finland, Norway and Sweden—June 1997

Travel does have an inexplicable way of drawing people into its fold and ingraining in them a spell of continuity. With each passing year, vacation getaways were becoming a compelling aspect of our lifestyles. When friends ask us—"Isn't it stressful planning vacations every year down to the minutest detail?"—my consistent reply is "On the contrary. We now look forward to making trips to distant corners of the world and to times when our lives get enriched in ways beyond verbal description." Today, I can certainly vouch for the fact that travel is not only a global classroom without borders, but also a genre beholden to widening human horizons. Mesmerizing coastlines, dizzying peaks, limitless vistas and history of mankind buffed and dented over time, only served to awaken the dormant domain of the human mind.

The Scandinavian nations of Denmark, Norway and Sweden along with Nordic Finland have been known to share a well-deserved reputation for nature's bounty, vivid folklore and a prosperous, cultivated people. Unlike most other sightseeing vacations that were geared to tourism at its best, this trip was projected to be modest on the wallet and more importantly, provide real insights into the lives, cultures and time honored traditions of their people. So Scandinavia it was going to be, the "Land of the Midnight Sun" where historic old world cities travel back in time to the Viking era.

In early June 1997, a Finnish airline flew us overnight into Helsinki from an eastern gateway in the U.S. Since we were slated to spend only a day there, our city tour commenced within hours of our arrival at the modest downtown Scandic Hotel. Helsinki, the "daughter of the Baltic," has been the capital of Finland since 1812. A city of half million residents, the prime practiced religion here continues to be Lutheran. As we headed towards the famous Temppeliankia (Rock Church), we found the pristine streets of Helsinki lined with tall domed cathedrals and Finland's indomitable Nordics walking briskly with ski poles in hand seemingly headed for a date with their popular cross-country sport. Our guide informed us that the Finnish people were originally an agrarian society with a deep-seated cultural heritage. Over time, they took to urban life style and today their standard of living is one of the highest in the world. Most Finns move to their vacation homes in the countryside in summer. Art exhibitions and musical extravaganzas form an integral part of life and living in Finland.

As we alighted at the entrance of the Temppelianka Church, it was at once obvious that this Lutheran church was very different from any we had ever seen. Built in 1969, this marvel of architecture was hewn from a single mound of rock and resembled a spaceship to those of us who had an extraordinary capacity for imagination. It had a concave copper dome roof lined with skylights. The inside of the church was even more far-removed from the traditional appearance. The church organ sat amidst quarried rocks and stones, and the jagged granite walls were silent witnesses to the process of erratic rock formation. There was no assigned altar. The pews carved from birch wood could seat over 500 people. This inspiring, functional church beckoned its faithful to prayer in a truly peaceful and secluded atmosphere. We halted at a Finnish restaurant for a typical meal consisting of fish and reindeer served with an abundance of potatoes, vegetables and bread. Superb taste and freshness made this traditional meal thoroughly enjoyable. We then headed to the must-see Olympic stadium of Helsinki where the statue of Paavo Nurmi (a venerated long distance runner of Finland) greeted us at the entrance. The mammoth stadium has a seating capacity of 40,000 at any given time. The 200-foot tower alongside provided tourists a vantage view of the city. After a short stop to view an outdoor sculpture by Finland's famous Ala Hiltonian, we returned to the hotel for dinner and hope of a good night's sleep. At that hour, it was still bright as daylight. I initially thought that our hotel had some sort of "special effects" lighting in place. But the concierge reminded us that we were in Finland, and Finland's sun, which graces the twilight sky all summer, does not dip beyond the horizon for too long. Darkness did set in for a short while and in the wee hours of the morning it was daylight again. The entire phenomenon was enough to induce in me an insomnia of sorts, stemming from an emotional mix of fascination, spookiness and fatigue.

The next morning we were on a one-and-a-half-hour flight to Copenhagen in neighboring Denmark. As always, the day of arrival in any city is a day of rest and socializing with our trip mates. Our waterfront hotel here was originally an ammunition garrison for the Danish navy but presently done up to its current décor, while still retaining some of the old world charm. The front lobby regaled with showcases displaying replicas of Danish warships and mounted battleship cannons.

Later in the day, some of us decided to stroll through Nyhaven, the colorful restored waterfront district, to meet the locals, because experience had taught us that an insider view of any culture is best seen through its people. The Danes came across as friendly people but busily went about their own business. Some of them stopped to smile or nod at an unfamiliar face. We had the good fortune of striking up a conversation with a Danish professor who seemed to be more than glad to talk to us. We learned from him that Christianity was an integral part of Danish life with leanings to the Lutheran church, and that Danes were very informal people who absolutely cherished and valued the concept of family life. There was no legal obligation to attend school in Denmark, though some form of education was mandatory, be it home schooling or special needs school or attending the regular public schools. Education was free of charge at the university level as well. Danish education, the professor went on to say, was based on democratic fundamentals where students retained the option to decide their own curriculum provided they were well within the requirements laid down by the law. My husband was curious to learn about their health care costs to determine how it compared with our system in the U.S. We were told that Denmark had a tax financed health care system which provided its citizens free access to medical care throughout their life span. At the end of an hour's conversation, we thanked the professor for his time and returned to our hotel with the satisfaction of an evening well spent.

Canal tours using multi-lingual guides were very popular in Copenhagen. We took this mode of transportation along the waterways and were ferried through the heart of the city to get to designated landmarks. Amalienborg Palace, the prime residence of the Danish Royal family, was our first stop. The palace was built around an octagonal square at the center of which was an equestrian statue of King Frederik V. Every noon when the royal family was in residence, the Danish royal guard marched through the city from the brick red Rosenborg Castle (which houses the crown jewels of the Danish monarchy) to the Amalienborg Palace for the "changing of the Guard" ceremony. Situated in the gardens of the palace grounds behind the Queen's residence was the Statue of Gideon, the Goddess of Earth who stood personified in an elaborate four-tiered monument.

After a short break for lunch consisting of pumpernickel sandwiches served with Danish meatballs and apple cobblers for dessert, we reached the Copenhagen harbor to view the statue of the Little Mermaid seated on a rock overlooking the sea. She apparently symbolized the fairy tale figure in Hans Christian Andersen's book which tells the story of a young mermaid who was prepared to sacrifice everything in order to achieve the love of a prince and ultimate immortality.

Our last stop for the day was the Tivoli Gardens, located in the heart of the city and listed among the most popular tourist destinations. Founded in 1843, it hosts an amusement park catering to young and old alike, an ancient pantomime theater, a concert hall, numerous cafes and a fascinating garden in full bloom with roses, mums, and tulips in every conceivable hue and shade. At sunset, the illuminated view of the gardens collectively reflected a magnificent display by day and an unforgettable sight by night. Copenhagen, situated on Scandinavia's warmest waters, was home to majestic castles, tranquil canals, heather-covered moors and upscale cafes. It was essentially a modern metropolis that had not permitted its history to slip into oblivion over the years.

The next morning's itinerary was a motor coach ride to Kronborg Castle at Elsinore about 30 miles away. Overlooking the bright blue waters where the North Sea and the Baltic Sea meet is an astonishing ensemble of pink sandstone walls topped with green towering minarets on well laid out lush lawns. Entrance to the castle on the cliffs of Elsinore is through a drawbridge on the moat. The ground floor housed the Maritime and Trade Museum and interestingly, we saw a niche in the castle yard dedicated to William Shakespeare who had immortalized this place by making it the venue for his play *Hamlet*. As we walked through sections of the castle on the upper floors the tour guide halted by the statue of a sleeping Danish hero—Holger Danske. He went on to narrate the legend that Danske never lost a battle in his life, but eventually got so homesick that he walked back to Denmark from Emperor Charles' court in south of France. Myth has it that if ever Denmark's sovereignty is threatened, Holger Danske would awaken to defend his country.

The basement of the castle, we were told, housed prison cells with just enough standing rooms for its inmates and was maintained at very low temperatures all year long as an additional torture tool.

We returned to the hotel for an afternoon's siesta and awaited the home hosted evening dinner with a Danish couple. This was to be the highlight of our stay in Copenhagen when we would get to learn firsthand the importance of family life in this culture and the proud traditions of the Danes. There were four host families listed for our entire group and that worked out to three guest couples per family. I had earlier on made a point of letting our tour guide know that my husband was a strict vegetarian, and requested that the information be relayed to our host. At the appointed hour, we were driven to our host's home. Even as we stepped out of the van, our gracious host and his wife were at the gate to extend us a warm welcome and escorted us along the brick walkway into their modest home. The host spoke with a rather heavy accent, taking care to introduce his wife first and then himself.

Next came viewing time of their family pictures displayed on the walls of the Victorian room. As we settled down to drinks served with a variety of nuts, the host stood up and asked: "Who is the vegetarian 'doktor' here?" My husband put up his hand classroom style. The gracious host assured him that his lovely wife and he had specially prepared a vegetarian salad for him. Shortly thereafter we were shown to the dining room where a service for eight was neatly laid out. My husband the vegetarian was assigned to the head of the table while the rest of us took our seats as shown. Our host and his wife brought out with great care a large vegetarian salad platter and set it before my husband. One glance in that direction and I let out an inaudible gasp! The salad was far from being vegetarian. It was done up in concentric circles, the outermost being cooked jumbo shrimp. The next row was made up of shredded lettuce and onions and a third row followed with cherry tomatoes and baby carrots. The pattern repeated itself to the point of a pyramid formation. I glanced sideways to see my husband's reaction to the shrimps. I noticed nothing alarming. He was busy thanking his host for all the trouble they went to on his account. The rest of us had to partake of a large platter of meat and potatoes fixed in Danish style and served with sourdough bread. The host reverentially chanted the "Grace" and we commenced dinner.

My husband ate his salad without demur, never for a moment letting on that he was raised in an orthodox Brahmin household in India where even eggs were taboo, where there was never a whiff of fish or seafood in the air, and where even a random mention of chicken or meat called for religious purification of the body and soul. He had continued to remain a vegetarian even after three decades of stay in the U.S. When dinner was done, my husband's platter was as empty as the rest of ours. I was pretty positive that he might have to make a beeline to the restroom pretty soon. But none of that occurred. Our hostess seemed pretty pleased with herself for having fixed the tasty "vegetarian meal." Dessert was served consisting of rice porridge with cream and vanilla and topped with hot cherry sauce. We had certainly enjoyed the inherent informality in a Danish home. There was nothing to indicate that they had gone to extraordinary lengths to fix a gourmet meal for us. But their warmth, hospitality and exuberance made the visit so worthwhile and memorable. As we bid goodbye, they gifted us boxed liquor glasses as souvenirs of our visit to Denmark.

On returning to our living quarters, I exclaimed to my husband, "You are a great big actor—claiming to be vegetarian and yet polishing off the seafood without batting an eyelid."

He paused for a moment and the replied, "I thought you would say I was a gentleman."

The word struck a deep chord within me and I replied, "Yes indeed. I do take back what I said."

He went on to further elaborate—"They put together

a vegetarian dish the best way they knew how. And I wasn't going to hurt their feelings in any form or fashion."

The following morning was a short stint to the Danish Queen's lavish summer castle at Frederiksborg. Built in red stone with traditional spires, it sat in manicured grounds amidst the azure waters of a lake. The colors could well have been right out of a painter's palette. In the evening, as we bid farewell to Copenhagen and our quaint hotel, we posed for a few pictures by the mounted cannons, fantasizing a twenty-one gun salute to ourselves. We were then transported to a mid-sized ship for an overnight cruise to Oslo, the capital city of neighboring Norway.

Oslo, which retains its original Viking name and is home to the Norwegian Royal Family, is believed to be one of the largest capital cities in the world and one of the most expensive as well. As we sailed on Norwegian waters, we could see the coastline dotted with green islands sporting picturesque summer homes and indented with beautiful fjords. A majestic ancient citadel in the distance stood spectacularly above the Oslo fjord. On disembarkation, which turned out to be a quick process, we were escorted to a centrally situated premier hotel on the main street of Oslo. The rooms were in European style, sound proof and clean, though way smaller in size than in U.S. hotels. We were assured of a noise-free atmosphere since that had always been an ongoing concern with tourists in that locale of bars and nightclubs.

After a quick brunch consisting of open-faced sandwiches, fish cakes, meat balls and cabbage, we set out sight-seeing with a local guide in attendance.

Akershus Castle, overlooking the harbor was our

first stop of the day. It was the medieval stronghold of Norway in the 13th century and was later turned into a Renaissance Castle. Housing the castle church, the Royal Mausoleum and elaborate banquet halls, it continued to be the focal point of the city's rich heritage. Our next stop was Oslo's pride and joy—the Vigeland Park which carried the lifework of sculptor Gustav Vigeland. As we entered this unique arena, we saw sculptures to the front of us and sculptures to the sides of us, envisaged in bronze, marble and stone depicting the different stages in the life of a mortal from birth to death. Lining the walkway to the central Monolith Pillar were edifices of men, women, and children, some encircled in bronze wheels to denote the ongoing cycle in human relationships. The Monolith Pillar itself was a mammoth column about fifty feet high around which were carved numerous entwined human figures, some seemingly lifeless at the base with others picking up vibrance higher up on the pillar, but all of them apparently yearning for the "Ultimate." What that ultimate would be was left to the imagination of the beholder—possibly resurrection or spirituality, or cycles of rebirth. What Vigeland had in mind when he sculpted them is anybody's guess. On either side of the Monolith were numerous granite figures projecting varying forms of human relationships. Some were men and women with a child between them, some of young couples in embrace, some of growing vibrant children and some of shriveled figures decrepit with old age.

Across from the gamut of sculptures was a large stone fountain sporting a huge basin shouldered by six giant sculptures taking on the water gushing onto them. The interpretation was that the men were toiling muscle, sinew and all with the burden of life while being doused with the flowing water that symbolized fertility. Edging

117

the parapet around the colossal fountain were groups of sculpted trees with human figures alongside, establishing man's inherent bondage with Nature. The nearby museum carried the early works of Vigeland in wood and his sketches in black and white. We next headed to the Viking Museum which gave us an insight into the Viking Age in the 9th century. On display were restored Viking ships recovered from the ocean floor of the Oslo Fjord.

We were told that Norwegians were avid skiers who frequented the ski slopes more than bars and cafes. Hence the popular saying in Norway that they are "born with skis on their feet." Sight-seeing in Oslo ended with a walk down Oslo's main shopping center—the Karl Johan's Gate. For centuries it had been the hub of Oslo with its charming cafes, galleries and feature shops. The most popular take home gifts among us were the traditional Norwegian hand knitted sweaters. Although expensive, they turned out to be a must. I picked up Troll dolls for casual gift giving.

The next morning we were to take a spectacular train ride on Norway's world famous Flam Railway from Oslo to Bergen. We arrived at Myrdal Station by motor coach to board the flaming red train. At an elevation of 2,840 feet, the Flam Valley descends steeply down towards Aurland Fjord going through several looped tunnels inside the mountains to cope with all of the 2,840 feet along a mere twelve-and-a-half-mile track. During the one hour descent, the uniquely designed train chugged through perilous landscape, past windswept mountain plateaus and ski slopes. Our emotions kept pace with the electrifying feel of the moment and the ecstasy of the sights and sounds around—miles of snow covered terrain hosting the cascading waterfalls, some of which were charging down at thunderous speed from dizzy mountain heights to taper into a dainty cloud of mist at the base, glacier covered ravines, and mighty gorges snaking their way through the forest region carrying in their wake plunging rivers. At times the snow clad peaks seemed to reach out to the blue skies with the horizons stooping in respectful obeisance. There were some skiers around who were still there past Easter in a traditional last salute to winter. We alighted at the Flam Railway station nestling in the innermost valley of Aurland Fjord, to take a two-hour luncheon cruise along the Sogne Fjord known to be "king of fjords" and the longest navigable fjord in the world. We were on board a small vessel since larger ships cannot negotiate the narrowing passages between the towering mountains.

If an artist were ever to capture the epitome of serenity, this was the dream scene. We cruised past bird sanctuaries and steep cliffs down which pristine waterfalls chose to make their descent. To any outdoor lover, the scenario could well echo the song of the fjords. Traditional Norwegian lunch was served on board, consisting of hot dogs (Polser in Norwegian) and bread, veggie sandwiches, and Potato Lefse—a Norwegian-style potato flat bread to be eaten with meatballs or jelly. Drinks and ice cream brought us full circle. Relaxing on deck chairs, we watched our little ship sail past the largest glacier in Europe—the "Blue Ice World" as they called it. Those were mesmerizing moments that one could relive through posterity. Back to the real world, we navigated past Norway's stunning coastal archipelago, past fields covered with wild flowers, and tiny hidden villages before disembarking at Gudvangen for our onward motor coach ride to Bergen.

This phase of the trip was no less breathtaking, with

a harmonious view of land, mountain and sea. The Flam Mountains dominated the panoramic landscape, while winding roads in the valleys below curved at the behest of Nature and cobalt waters graced the indented coastlines. There were a few hairy moments however when the huge motor coach swerved to negotiate hairpin bends.

Bergen city was sprawled out along the mountainsides with quaint wooden homes perched between rocks. We were accommodated in a guesthouse apartment in the center of the city, within walking distance of the funicular and the world famous fish market. Bergen, also known as the "Gateway of Fjords," is a renowned fishing center and Norway's largest port of call for cruise ships, accounting for the large influx of tourists here. Whole blocks of ancient white wooden houses stood along the cobbled streets serving as keepsake memories of yesteryears. We found most Norwegians biking to their destinations and those who chose to drive automobiles did not believe in honking. Norway was destitute during the Viking Era but their fortunes turned around significantly in the late 1960s when they struck oil big time and today they are the third largest oil exporters in the world. The wealthiest Norwegians pay over 50 percent in taxes, we were told. They certainly could live like royalty, but that would not be in keeping with the Norwegian thought process. Hiking and fishing are popular pastimes in this country though we did not get to try our hand at them for paucity of time. Our guide enlightened us on the Norwegian system of education. Between the ages of six and sixteen basic education was free and mandatory. Private schools are not popularly patronized and allowed to exist only if they are of a religious denomination. We also learned that women have a strong presence in public life, comprising one-third of the Parliament and 40 percent of the country's labor force.

A one-and-a-half-hour flight brought us into Stockholm—a beautiful city situated on the sparkling waters across four islands and the stunning capital of Sweden. We were settled into a comfortable quarter of the Scandic chain of hotels in the shopping district. We spent the day of arrival in walking through the immaculate streets where for the first time we heard a bevy of foreign languages spoken, including Bengali, my mother tongue. We saw well preserved ancient buildings standing alongside modern high rises and ornately lit buildings projecting the ultimate in Scandinavian beauty. Friendly Swedes stopped to greet us in the cosmopolitan buzz. We managed to spot an Indian restaurant in the area and lost no time patronizing it. We were greeted at the entrance with a traditional "namaste" followed by "valkommen" which in Swedish means "welcome."

The next morning we set out to view the royal palaces around Stockholm, and they took us back in time through Swedish history. The red stone Gripsholm Castle, on the banks of Lake Maleren, was built by Gustav Vasa in the 1500s reflecting architecture that span 400 years of bygone eras. The Swedish royal palace, also called Kungliga Slottet, located in old town, was the official residence of King Carl XVI Gustav. Unlike most of the castles in Scandinavia, this massive barrack-like structure on the waterfront had niches in the walls that carried classical Roman statues. There were an overwhelming number of rooms, which housed royal jewelry and medieval armor. I recall this edifice with ease because of its unconventional appearance and the fact that it had one room more than Buckingham Palace!

We were on the road again, headed for the prized stop of the day—a tour of the Stockholm Concert Hall and the City Hall. It was the venue where the coveted Nobel Awards were given out on Dec. 10th each year to recognize those who had through their contributions, striven for betterment of humanity or progress in science. Referring to the history of the Nobel Prize, the guide told us that Alfred Nobel had made his fortune with the discovery of dynamite. He wanted it to be used for peaceful causes and carved for himself a place in eternity by instituting the awards as his lifetime legacy. He passed away on December 10th, 1896 and the awardees for medicine, literature, physics, chemistry and economics (the last category was instituted by the Nobel Committee a few decades ago) are recognized on that day by the King of Sweden to commemorate the life of a genius and philanthropist. The Nobel Peace Prize, however, is awarded in Oslo by the King of Norway. Following the awards ceremony in Stockholm, the recipients are honored at a lavish banquet with a spread of Swedish and Nordic cuisines. Our orientation ended as we alighted at the City Hall. We walked around the hallowed buildings graced by luminaries each year on December 10th—the Blue Room, the Golden Room and the reception area, all of which seemed to come alive with academic grace. While our trip mates ambled around in a dream world of their own, I chose to stand at the entrance of the imposing Blue Room and have my picture taken. In my mind, that was as close as I would get to any Nobel Prize in this life!

During our ride back to the hotel, our tour guide familiarized us with life in Sweden. The Swedes, he said, were very health conscious people like the rest of Scandi-

The entrance to the Blue Room where the reception for Nobel Laureates is held in Stockholm

navia and indulged in jogging, biking and skiing for physical fitness. Education was free and Swedish citizens had lifetime access to public medical services. Sweden was a monarchy and a democracy that recognized the powers of the common man.

Midsummer's Festival was a celebrated holiday in the country. Stemming from ancient pagan rituals, the Swedes observe it with drinking and merry-making around a garlanded maypole.

We retired early since the following day was going to be a busy one with visits to the Vasa Museum and the historic university town of Uppsala, located an hour from Stockholm. We found ourselves in the first tour batch inside the Vasamuseet. Situated on the island of Djurgarden, this museum houses the Vasa, a wooden royal warship that went down in Stockholm waters during her maiden voyage in 1628. She was salvaged, resurfaced and reassembled to completion after 333 years. The entire tour of the ship was in dim lighting with a distinctly musty feel. Haunting tales were narrated in between displays of salvage operations, and they only served to heighten spookiness in those of us who were all ears for eerie sights or sounds. After a much-needed stop for lunch in an open-air eatery, we were headed to Uppsala, labeled as the cradle of Swedish civilization.

Uppsala is a quaint town and home to the oldest existing university in the world. The Uppsala Domkyrka, believed to be Scandinavia's largest cathedral, stands on the ruins of ancient heathen temple of the 13th century. Built in Gothic style, it houses the tomb of King Gustav Vasa. The new cathedral and seat of the Archbishop of Sweden is a towering edifice with a futuristic look. Its interior décor is in Tiffany style with a raised pulpit ornately carved in wood and gold. Across from the imposing Uppsala cathedral is the Gustavianum built in 1625 as the seat of the university. The present newer university buildings in Italian Renaissance style were constructed in the mid 1980s across the Gustavianum. At the Uppsala university library, popularly known as Carolina Rediviva, we got to see a page out of the Silver Bible handwritten in Gothic in the 6th century and considered to be their most treasured exhibit. The story, however, goes that the Silver Bible seen here is not the entire manuscript and that parts of it are concealed in the Swedish mountain regions. Next on the itinerary was a visit to the three Royal Burial Mounds located a couple of miles away at Gamla Uppsala. It was an established site of heathen worship and rituals and history has it that every 8th year during full moon, the heathen culture demanded a daily sacrifice of eight males—one human and seven animals for eight consecutive days. Being hung from holy trees was the accepted mode of sacrifice. Narration of these ghoulish facts by the guide seemed to draw a beleaguered and uneasy silence amongst us. Unperturbed, however, he continued his expositions of 6th century royal burials. It was believed at the time, that a dead king cremated in his armor would reach Valhalla through the consuming fire. The remains were then interred under cobblestones, gravel and sand. Royalty were honored with mounds similar to those in front of us. I quickly shifted my gaze to the distant landscape for mental relief but the undulating land amidst hillocks presented the same curvy look as those mounds facing us. Possibly there were miles of mounds big and small, leading me to believe that we were standing smack in the middle of a burial site. Our ride back home saw us in a somber mood, while we tried to come to grips with the guide's interpretation of the pagan culture.

The "Farvaal" banquet that evening marked the culmination of the Scandinavian Odyssey and we prepared to depart for Helsinki the following morning to board our international flight back to the United States.

Twelve

Tahiti—Hawaii Cruise: Tahitian and Hawaiian Islands— October 1998

In mid-1998, I once again donned my traveler's hat to plan a vacation to a destination with a difference. Indelible memories detailing where we had been and what we had seen over the years had created in us a passion for travel that took priority over all else and a preference for comfort and global savvy.

We were focusing on a unique getaway to a remote and yet exotic location beyond the realm of cell phones and laptops, a retreat where we could relive a semblance of our childhood days in a third world country. I could not come up with any suggestions short of journeying to our hometown of Chennai in South India. But even there urbanization and information technology had arrived to make a permanent presence. Gone were the days when the milkman showed up at the crack of dawn to milk his cow at our doorstep under my mother's vigilant supervision, when barbers arrived before breakfast to render in-home service to the men folk, when mailmen in khaki uniforms (we called them postmen) trudged the dusty roads braving the scorching sun or pouring rain to deliver mail, and when cars, refrigerators and telephones were still status symbols to middle class families. While we were still pondering on possible vacation locales over dinner, the telephone rang. It was an overseas call from a former trip mate who had kept in touch with us over the years. His suggestion turned out to be the absolute answer to our quest for a travel destination.

Sailing off the beaten track to South Pacific's Society Islands on a Princess Cruise—Tahiti to Hawaii, with dockings at Moorea, Bora Bora, Kiribati (Christmas Island) and the Hawaiian Islands would be a dream vacation, he said. We would even be awarded "Merit Certificates" for crossing the Equator! He would not be able to accompany us this time, but journeying to these remote Polynesian Islands would indeed be a surreal experience. In a heartbeat, our minds were made up and we embarked on travel plans for October 1998. Tahiti was a land of elemental beauty, a name that instantly conjured up the aesthetic legacies of Paul Gauguin, the evergreen rain forests that played hosts to generations of exotic flora and fauna, the mountains covered with glistening raindrops, and the life of the Polynesians in their peaceful and unhurried atmosphere.

On October 5th, 1998, we flew out of a western gateway in the U.S. on a chartered ten-hour flight into Papeete, the capital town of Tahiti. It was the largest of the 118 islands of French Polynesia, sprawled over 400 square miles. As our flight cautiously started its descent into Tahiti, we could see black sand beaches bordering the lagoons, silver lined clouds capping the mountain peaks and dense forests rising amidst the emerald green valleys.

After a picture-perfect landing and completion of brief customs formalities, we were welcomed with flower garlands and fresh fruit juice in traditional Tahitian style. We were then escorted to our ocean liner docked in the adjacent Papeete Harbor. This residential cruise ship was a whopping 800 feet long with a passenger capacity of 1750 and a crew of 700. We were shown to a well appointed outside cabin with a private balcony. The interior was cherry-wood paneled and the drapes in pastel shades completed the décor. The layout was similar to but larger than the cruise ships we had sailed earlier. There were over a dozen decks at different levels hosting conference centers, casinos, cocktail lounges, beauty salons and spas, sport and fitness facilities, and walk-around promenades. Selected dining areas required their guests to be in formal attire for the evening dinner, while other eateries catered to passengers who preferred a more informal ambience. A welcome added feature on this floating palace were poolside movie screens for outdoor viewing of movies while relaxing on the lounge chairs. We spent the day settling into our cabin, getting our picture IDs and exploring the ship's layout.

On the first evening aboard the ship which was still docked, was the formal "Welcome dinner" in the banquet hall. Men were in tuxedoes and ladies in glittering evening gowns. I, as always, chose to show up in a sari and this time it was beige pure silk woven with jacquard paisleys in peach and gold. The captain was the first to compliment me, followed by many others. To them it obviously was a very different kind of evening gown.

We had seated ourselves at the assigned tables when all heads turned towards the doorway. A tall, beautiful lady in a black taffeta ballroom dress gracefully walked in. Random stray curls highlighted her sand brown coiffure, while her large eyes, slightly upturned nose and dimple cheeks were attestations to an erstwhile era of ravishing beauty. Her delicate diamond necklace and her long shimmering earrings visibly enhanced her glamour. The regal air about her undoubtedly suggested a lineage

The author in the foyer of the ship *Crown Princess* on the Tahiti Cruise

of aristocracy. As it turned out, her seating happened to be at our table, next to me. Outgoing by disposition, she lost no time getting to know her tablemates. Her name, which I forget now, sounded Austrian or Swedish. In conversation we learned that she was a countess by birth. She seemed extremely fascinated with my sari—the texture, the color and the get-up. Very politely, she asked me if I could arrange to get her 100 yards of the exact same material. I hastened to explain to her that saris came in lengths of six or nine yards and the particular one I was wearing was a six-yard designer sari. My rendering of the situation did not seem to have any effect on her. She still wanted 100 yards of this particular sari material. I then suggested that if she compromised on the color and design, maybe rolls of pure silk in solid colors could be ordered for her in India. But no, she wanted 100 yards of this exact same sari. Finally I made bold to ask her what she intended to use it for. With a faint smile and a seemingly resigned look, she replied—"I want it for drapes in my castle." It left me dumbfounded for the rest of the evening. I remember this incident so distinctly because exposure to absurdity can sometimes leave a lasting imprint on memory. I did run into this lady occasionally on the cruise but stayed clear of any reference to a sari.

All of the following day was dedicated to a detailed tour of Papeete. Tahiti Nui Travels drove us in the comfort of an air-conditioned motor coach down Boulevard Pomare—the primary three-lane thoroughfare along the city's waterfront. We saw neat, sheltered bus stops carrying large city maps with the scenic beauty of Tahiti as a backdrop. Modern apartment buildings and shopping high rises lined the roads in the heart of the city. At no point did the ocean fade out of sight. We were headed to

Gauguin's Museum to see a display of Paul Gauguin's masterpieces and exhibits dedicated to his life in French Polynesia. The exterior of the Museum looked unpretentious, with clusters of sugarcane and banana plants dotting the courtyard. Nearby was an ancient bus stop—an apology for a shelter, which stood on four posts of decaying timber holding up a thatched roof. It served as a stark reminder of Gauguin's frugal times. Paul Gauguin was born in 1848 in France and arrived in Tahiti in 1891 to make it his beloved home. He died unrecognized and penniless on the Marquesan Island of French Polynesia in 1903. He spent over ten years in Tahiti after realizing that the indigenous, charming locals rendered new dimensions to his spiritual take on art. His masterpiece in Synthetist style was "The Yellow Christ" while some of the other famed works were "Two Women on the Beach" and "The Tahitian Landscape." Eye-catching among the displays was the recreation of the doorway that Gauguin had painted on his own island home.

Our guide went on to educate us on the works and style of Gauguin's close friend Vincent Van Gogh, without mention of whom a portrayal of Gauguin would be incomplete. Van Gogh was a troubled Dutch painter and genius. Expressionism in color was his style and his stormy life and mental anguish came alive in his works of art. His masterpiece "The Starry Night over the Rhone" was painted in deep dark colors during one of his phases of despair and depression. His last painting "Wheat Field with Crows" did reflect a foreboding of his untimely end at thirty-seven years of age. The roads in the painting led to nowhere and crows spelt an omen of bad luck to him. He shot himself in the very wheat field that he had just completed on canvas.

The gift shop adjacent to the museum carried beautiful reproductions of Gauguin's paintings which were a lot more affordable than the originals. We bought one of "Two Women on the Beach" depicting native charm that vibrantly sprung alive from the brushes of a maestro.

We next drove past the Vaimahuta Falls in the rain forests of Tahiti. Cascading from dizzying heights spraying a white mist of gossamer, it was as close to a bridal veil as Mother Nature would permit. We then traveled to the site of the lighthouse Point Venus overlooking Matavi Bay. The Tahara Mountain Ranges in the background contributed for the most part in making the panoramic view absolutely breathtaking. Captain James Cook was believed to have first landed here during his circumnavigation around the world between 1768 and 1771. It was way past noon when we stopped at a wayside restaurant for a quick bite to eat—the choices being lobster, chicken, vegetarian sandwiches and potato fries.

The crowning event of the day was a visit to the Tahiti Pearl Museum, which specialized in South Sea Black Pearls. The women hurriedly got off the bus and forged ahead towards the museum while the spouses followed wryly, anticipating a sizable damage to their wallets. To own a natural black pearl was bound to be any woman's dream! The museum official enlightened us on the history of the black pearls, how they are cultured and features to look for before making a selection. Black pearls in showcases were displayed in different sizes and shapes. Most of them were mounted as pendants, rings and earrings. My husband had already started scanning the ones with the cheaper price tags. But I had my heart set on a ring carrying a good size natural, iridescent black pearl. It was going to be this or nothing. My husband meekly submitted to the unspoken command because years of marriage had taught him the futility of negotiations in such situations. Most of the womenfolk returned to the motor coach, agog with smiles while the spouses mentally tried to reconcile to the inevitable dip in their bank balances.

We were back in our cabins by evening, preparing to sail out at dawn. The usual fetish of fire drill and life jacket rehearsals were completed in due course and at daybreak we were at sea headed twelve miles west of Tahiti to the tranquil island paradise of Moorea. The ship was docked at a permissible mooring distance in the sea and we were transported to shore by "tenders" (little motorized boats). The warm, friendly Polynesians welcomed us with garlands to the singing of lilting island melodies while young damsels in grass skirts swayed with synchronization and grace, performing a native dance. Watching the morning sun rise amidst the haunting peaks of the island was spiritual, to say the least. We traveled on foot to explore Moorea's pristine beauty accentuated by white sand beaches and coral reefs. The gracious and inviting locals grimaced in glee as we stopped to buy their handicrafts—hand woven fruit baskets, little seashell bowls and cowry chains. Numerous "Moutus" (little islands formed by waves and winds pushing the coral reef up on itself) dotted the area. Rows of thatched huts on stilts in the waters were the location for our picnic luncheon. We had a choice of grilled seafood, sushi, and vegetable platters. Fresh island fruits like mangoes and lychees were served for dessert. Our physical hunger seemed to pale into insignificance in the face of the prodigal beauty that Nature presented—the palm fringed coasts and the crystal clear waters of the emerald lagoons. Magnificent underwater views of the coral gardens were an added bonus. Most of us experienced a sense of peace that fine-tuned the spirituality of the inner being.

We drove past luxuriant valleys, which were home to

lush plantations and halted briefly at Belvedere Point for pictures of Mount Rotui looming large in the background. Back to our ship by evening, we set sail north-east for an overnight passage to Bora Bora—one of the most captivating islands in the Pacific Ocean and a favored destination for honeymooners. Located 150 miles from Tahiti, it is known as the "Pearl of the Pacific." The lagoons ranged in colors from emerald green to cobalt blue, and the unrelenting ocean waves battered the foamy coasts for miles on end. As with all South Pacific island moorings, we were transferred to shore by "tenders." The choppy waters, which sometimes got menacingly choppier, forced us to turn our gazes every now and then towards the location of life jackets. Our Polynesian tour guide, unmindful of the swaying and rocking of the tender, continued filling us in on the origin of Bora Bora. Volcanic to begin with, this island was formed from the eroded remnants of a crater. We learned that Mount Otemanu and Mount Pahia continue to be the two black volcanic peaks that still dominate the lush green island.

On arrival in Bora Bora we were escorted to a five star hotel for an island breakfast. The imposing entrance to the hotel was in keeping with the ambience of the island—large conical thatched roofs over the lobby, towering palm trees and multihued hibiscus bowers lining the walkways, and graceful, brown-skinned Tahitian beauties with flower headgears and garlands waiting to accord us a traditional welcome. After a short break, we set out to explore mythical Bora Bora. The peace and bounty prevailing here were precursors to an unknown serenity. Life suddenly seemed to turn simple and uncomplicated. Maybe it was the remote location in the middle of nowhere with the dizzying whiffs of floral fragrance, or the even keel of life of the uncomplaining Polynesians, or possibly the virgin tread into an age-old past of mountains, valleys and oceans. Be that as it may, walking through this haven of bestowed splendor I was reminded of the words of poet Milton in his "Nativity Ode":

Time will run back and fetch the age of gold!

We drove past the magical lagoon at Anau Bay. It was a vivid presentation of colors in shades of blue that seemed to want to take turns to merge into the emerald green with little concern of losing their identity in the merger. The majestic peak at Matira Point chiseled to its present form by ancient volcanoes, towered over a shimmering lagoon of gemlike brilliance. Such tantalizing beauty explains why Bora Bora is considered the paradise of the Pacific Islands. We were delighted to be treated to a Tahitian feast on the beachfront while native dancers performed for us. We watched homebound boats on the ocean, seabirds coming home to nest, and crabs dominating the sands in liberal numbers. The native cuisine cooked in an "ahima" (underground oven) was a spread of roast pig, breadfruit, plantains, taro leaves and island fruits. The breadfruit dish, the bananas and the taro were delectable. We barely managed to keep the profile of the headless roasted pig away from our gaze. Fresh pineapple juice concluded the meal. On our way back to the ship, we were shown quaint, high-end restaurants—some sporting a bamboo exterior, some with sand-bottom floors, and some nestling in bowers of tropical vegetation. I, for my part, was anxious to get back to the ship and relax in the comfort of our cabin.

Our ocean voyage in the true sense of the term actually commenced when we sailed out of Bora Bora and headed north towards Kiribati (Christmas Island) 1,200 miles away. The next few days were going to be spent at sea when stretches of oceanic beauty would possibly interface with the seemingly endless horizon. Tahiti, Moorea and Bora Bora—the very names brought back to us memories of an idyllic haven that could never be traded for scenic beauty that the rest of the world might offer.

Relaxation on the ship was the ultimate indulgence—there were no schedules to keep or buses to catch. We had more time to unwind, more time to connect with like-minded travelers, and more time to cherish the ever-changing scenic tapestry. Sunrise in the distant horizon, clouds of screeching seagulls flying past us hastily with an agenda of their own, and the captivating sunset in glowing shades of orange and yellow are sights that do not elude memory. The ship's crew went above and beyond the call of duty in waiting on their guests—some of whom were pleasant, some finicky and some demanding to the point of being outright rude. We patronized the four open seating restaurants as also the eatery that offered Chinese, Thai and Indian dishes under the banner of "Asian fusion cuisine." Formal dining in the evenings was an option but not a must. We spent a lot of time reading books, lazing on the sun-soaked decks, bidding at auctions of oil paintings and watching television to keep up with news of home. Occasional sightings of flipper dolphins and humpback whales in the distant waters provided transient excitement. At the end of three days of sailing, there was a shipboard announcement informing passengers that we were nearing Kiribati Islands, and that when the ship anchored in mid-sea, passengers intending to go ashore would be transported by tenders. Further announcements also alerted us to the fact that those who were likely to feel disturbed at the dire poverty on the island, were advised to stay back on the ship. My husband and I saw no reason not to go since we had lived in a third world country at one time and no extent of poverty could be that alarming to us. In casual conversation, we learned that Kiribati (aka Christmas Island) was named so since Captain Cook had landed there on Christmas Eve in 1777, and that ancestor worship and belief in ghosts and spirits were still prevalent on the island in spite of the advent of literacy and education. The local Gilbertese folks were apparently aquatic naturals—as adept in the ocean as they were on land. Coconut plantations and fishing were their primary source of income and basic subsistence was all that life afforded them.

This native island presented as an endless stretch of coral beaches with coconut palms and island shrubs serving to break the monotony. The locals welcomed us with flower garlands and tender coconut juice, as was their practice. The coconut water instantly called for a debate—to drink or not to drink. Eventually indulgence got the better of us and using our straws, we lapped up the refreshing drink from the innermost depths of the green fruit. Alongside a tribal dance was in progress. Native performers decked with flowers, cowry shells and grass skirts swayed in unison with outstretched arms to the beat of Hawaiian music while their distant gazes seemed to encapsulate the beyond. Encircling them were others singing, clapping and stomping to the beats of a rising crescendo. Little thatched stations on the beach were trading island handicrafts made of grass, straw and seashells. There was one stall however that feigned a more serious mission, labeled "The Post Office." We bought a picture postcard that was less doused in sand than others and mailed it to ourselves in the U.S., using the quaint native stamps on display. To this day the card hasn't arrived, granted that it had to ride the ocean waves to American soil.

As we walked the dirt roads on the island, we saw stray mongrels, carefree and owner-free using their olfactory senses to track down morsels of discarded food, hens and chickens wandering in gay abandon, and low thatched huts put together with logs, twine and palm fronds. These one-room abodes on tiny plots of land were the only dwelling places that this indigent community could afford. Coconut palms were the affordable decor that these little yards could boast of. A few prefabricated buildings served as stores and government offices. The concept of privacy obviously could not exist in a setup where everything was heard and seen. It was humbling to see the natives' graceful acceptance of life as it came to them. The men went ocean fishing and toddy tapping up the coconut trees while the women skillfully wove mats for beddings. They had for generations successfully maintained their traditional beliefs. The elders were looked upon as the sole cultural link to the past and regarded as icons of transition from one world to the next. Coconut toddy, known as "karewe" in Polynesian parlance, was their national drink while a meal normally consisted of cooked fish with baked taro (a starch tuber), breadfruit and papaya. As we walked past the tiny homes, I was intrigued to see little raised mounds in front of most homes. I asked the island guide what it signified in Polynesian culture. He replied: "Those mounds are the grave sites of the dead. People are too poor to afford a cemetery. And so they bury their dead by the front doorstep." I was speechless. Verses from Thomas Gray's "Elegy Written in a Country Churchyard" were an immediate flashback:

Beneath those rugged elms, that yew tree's shade,
Where heaves the turf in many a mouldering heap
Each in his narrow cell for ever laid,
The rude Forefathers of the hamlet sleep.

Perhaps in this neglected spot is laid
Some heart once pregnant with celestial fire;
Hands, that the rod of empire might have swayed,
Or waked to ecstasy the living lire.

We continued exploring the island on foot and I could see that the inner recesses were steeped in even greater poverty and squalor. The figure of an anguished woman sitting with a sick child on her lap outside her hutment caught my attention. As I went closer, it broke my heart to see the despair in the eyes of a dying toddler's mother, realizing that in the next few hours a young life was going to slip away—all for want of awareness, food, sanitation, immunization and medical care. Their nearest hospital was in Tahiti, barring a basic clinic in Bora Bora. The natural human element of compassion prompted me to offer her some monetary help. But at that late stage, dollar bills were not going to bring her child back. Maybe a few words of comfort and a gentle hug would have been in order in that inconsolable situation. But even that avenue was closed to me since I did not speak the native language, nor was I familiar with the island practices. I gave to her all I had—a prayer and a tear and moved on across the punished terrain of Kiribati. We returned to the ship, downcast and depressed, and probably more aware than ever that at the inevitable hour, Death the great leveler makes no distinction between the Manor born and the squalor born.

In the evening hours we set sail, headed to the Hawaiian Islands which constituted the last phase of this voyage. Christmas Island was located midway between Tahiti and Hawaii and that meant three more days at sea in this residential cruise ship. We watched the horizon gather storm—intimidating dark clouds racing through the skies, tiny little stars trying to make a reappearance in the moonless sky after the rains had abated, choppy waves lashing onto the sides of the ship in foaming wrath, and snatches of lightning playing second fiddle to Mother Nature's orgies. Far from the shores of the "madding crowds," we indulged in endless hours of relaxation, enjoyed the uncompromising hospitality of the shipboard crew, and savored the varying cuisines in nautically inspired settings. Nonetheless, the timeless seascape was getting to me and I yearned to tread on habited land again. We waited to set eyes on a populated world that seemed to have slipped away so innocuously. The Hawaiian Islands, we were told, constituted Paradise on earth where the gray jagged rocks would whisper to mortals in the whistling breeze, where the nimble island beauties would beckon their visitors with an enchanting "aloha," and where the soaring lush rain forests would indulge in preserving the pristine beauty in their bosoms, much like a mother does her precious offspring.

With our ship moored again in the mid-Pacific at dawn, we were "tendered" to Kauai, the smallest but oldest of the four major islands. A single volcano was believed to have caused the formation of this island measuring about 33 x 25 miles. With just a day at our disposal to explore this haven of beauty, we set out in a motor coach where every passenger had the luxury of a full-length window to view the stunning island scenery. From bridges across the rain forests, we saw fern grottos, lush tropical sanctuaries, taro fields cultivated in patches of greens in the verdant Hanalei valley, and breadfruit and guava groves planted with astonishing precision. The sea cliffs of the Na Pali coast towered like mute guards over the island, while African tulip trees with orange-red blooms brought in constant bursts of color. At the Arohoho point on Kauai beach, we witnessed an intrinsic scene of oceanic beauty. When the exposed lava flow meets the sea, waves reach into a lava tube and send a column of water through the rock into a blowhole resulting in spectacular jets of mist. Ethereal beauty of this island was indeed its reigning monarch. Little wonder then that the movies *Jurassic Park, Raiders of the Lost Ark* and *Blue Hawaii* were shot on location here. Although exposed to the ravages of erosion and the elements, Kauai still manages to present a magnificent vista.

After a brief stopover for sandwich and soda—our appetites took a back seat in the face of such bewitching beauty—we headed to the Waimea Canyon State Park. En route, we stopped at an outlook point for a view of the Waimea Canyon—a huge chasm of red and orange, in bold contrast to the green island backdrop. In the park, we walked down fern bedecked trails with pelicans and herons eyeing us warily, through forests of spruce and birch haunted by the buzz of insects and shrill bird calls from up above. An occasional moose or jungle fowl sprinted across our paths. Conical clusters of rare native flowers, purple orchids, wild Hawaiian plants and stretches of red and white hibiscus lent much needed color to the landscape. Our feet were pretty tired at the end of the trail run and we looked forward to returning to the ship.

Back at sea again, an overnight sailing brought us to

141

Maui for a predawn disembarkation. We were to savor the small town charm as the island awoke to its earthly splendor. Maui, also known as the "valley isle," is the second largest of the Hawaiian Islands covering over 700 square miles. The landscape here magically changed in front of our eyes—layers of passing clouds, brief drizzles followed by appearance of vibrant rainbows, and finally an exhilarating view of the sunrise in the distant horizon behind the 10,000 ft Haleakala Crater. The island was named for demigod Maui who according to legend cast his fishing line and pulled up this entire island out of the sea.

After a sumptuous breakfast comprising of Western and oriental cuisine and luscious island fruits, we were driven to the smaller west section of Maui which is connected to the larger section by a narrow isthmus. Our guide advised us that we would be concentrating on the west side only since it was a short day trip, but he promised us unprecedented and awe-inspiring views ahead. During our ride towards the Iao Valley State Park, the guide briefly walked us through the history of this ancient volcanic island. Polynesians were the original settlers here and in late 1700s, King Kamehameha conquered the Maui army in the Battle of Kepaniwai at the Iao Valley site. The remains of some of the high-ranking chiefs were believed to be in secret burial sites in the valley. The culture of this Aloha state underwent transformation with the arrival of God fearing missionaries in the 1800s. They introduced literacy, frowned on the "hula" and attempted to clothe Polynesian maidens conservatively while still retaining the free spirit of the island. He went on to explain that the hula or native Hawaiian dancing originated with the earliest Polynesian inhabitants. It was believed that when danced to musical chants they could represent a variety of situations—celebrations, warfare, rituals and practice of Hawaiian life. The smallest mistake in a hula dance could be a forecaster of bad luck, death or dishonor. But in today's world, hula is considered a gyrating and tantalizing dance form performed by native girls in grass skirts and coconut shell bras. I personally felt reprieved for my ignorance because I had no clue of its erstwhile honored position in the island culture. Although time did not permit us to visit Haleakala Peak, we learned that it has been a long dormant volcano with deeply burrowed valleys and steep ravines. Miles of sugarcane and pineapple plantations covered the slopes of the crater. The crater itself could apparently compare in size to Manhattan Island in the U.S. Inside the crater district of Haleakala National Park is the Waikamoi Reserve, which the guide described as "God's Land where Time forever stands still." 200-year-old plants have been found in this lava covered gorge. Bird watchers could have a field day here with rare varieties like Maui parrot bill and the crested "akohekohe" frequenting the valley for food. Hawaiian mint plants and the rare tree geraniums also have a home here.

The lecture session ended in time for us to get off at Iao Valley State Park. The verdant surroundings abounded in exotic tropical plants, clusters of taro, hibiscus and palms of every known species. We followed the paved pathway across the streams and through the trails, stopping for pictures at dramatic overlooks of the Iao Needle—a 2000-foot rock pinnacle towering over lush terrain. It was awesome to be in full view of this geological marvel covered with green vegetation. The locals believe that Kanaloa, the Hawaiian God of the ocean, is represented by the phallic form of the Iao Needle.

Our next stop was the "Tropical Gardens of Maui."

The marine enthusiasts and snorkeling and scuba diving gurus headed to Molokoni Island—a crater emerging from the sea and home to a wealth of marine life. En route to the tropical gardens, we saw an abundance of the native shrub "pukiawe" in shades of green and pink. At the tropical gardens, we boarded an open tramcar for a ride through the plantations displaying the island specialties. We saw the exotic silver sword plant typical to Maui with several purple blossoms on large stalks. These flower only once in their lifetime ranging from five to twenty years and then they wither away. There were regular ferns growing to tree heights, the bougainvillea bowers sprawled in myriad hues, coconut groves and palm trees lining the walkways for those who had adequate stamina to do the entire tour on foot, the "ti" plants with their glowing ruby-red leaves, and the large ginger bushes with red Oapuhi blooms. All species were systematically labeled for the benefit of the non-botanist. Even these short stints in the comfort of a tramcar were exhausting since the relentless tropical sun kept us thirsty all the while.

On our way back to the ship, we briefly halted at an observation pavilion near the Kanaha Pond wildlife sanctuary where night herons returned to nest. We did get a glimpse of the rare Hawaiian Stilt, which sported orange legs rather than an orange plume. With a long day behind us, we waddled back to our ship and headed straight to the shower for warm soaks to our tired feet.

Before long, there was an announcement on the public address system reminding all passengers that the Captain's Farewell Dinner was going to be held that night in view of the fact that we would be offloaded at Hilo on the Big Island, the next morning. The entire day there would be ours to spend as we wished and in the evening we were to board a commercial airliner which would fly us back to the U.S. from the international airport at Hilo. Since formal attire was expected at this dinner, my husband resorted to his tuxedo and I to my sari, which this time around was an off-white silk with motifs of tiny elephants in turquoise and gold. I fervently hoped it would not be targeted again for castle drapes! As we entered the banquet hall of the ship, each of us was handed a "Certificate of Crossing the Equator," the interestingly worded contents of which I shall detail at the end of this chapter. An awesome display of the chef's handiworks was in a highlighted section of the hall: what looked like a yellow bowl of roses was actually custard in a clear glass bowl with roses crafted out of pink and yellow melons and lettuce leaves for the filling. An ancient church was immaculately crafted and sculptured from white cheese. There was a true to life windmill made of wheat thins, a fruit basket with an intricate weave carved in ice, an attractive green bird perched inside a niche in the watermelon, and many more such creative delights. The cameras lit up the area to capture these artistic presentations on film. The lure of mouthwatering delicacies could not be resisted for long and in time, the dance floor became the focus of revelers. As the evening wore on, the Hawaiian band struck up, embodying the spirit of the island. We waited our turn for a farewell handshake with the Captain and his crew, and later bid our shipmates good-bye as well. The protocol of getting our suitcases out in the hallway by midnight, for final disembarkation, had over the years become a familiar procedure. The good times were going to end soon as do all good things in life.

At daybreak we got off the ship at Hilo, which was located on the east side of the Big Island of Hawaii. Accommodation for the day in a resort hotel had been arranged ahead. After breakfast we set out with a local guide on a tour of Hilo. The past and present here seemed to fuse together to give it a mystical quality. We had planned on a half-day hike through the rain forest for a close-up view of the Akaka Falls (fourteen miles north of Hilo), plunging 400 feet through dense tropical vegetation. As we drove down the boulevards of Hilo lined with banyan trees for miles on end, native islanders waved out to us in warm welcome. Their gestures clearly emanated from the inner recesses of their beings. These were people whose lives revolved around resilience and resourcefulness, which unfolded each day to eventually write their history in a nation's journal. "Aloha" was not just another word to them; it was indeed their way of life.

As we drove on, we realized how privileged we were to witness the sights and sounds of God's own land—water sculpted landscapes, steep sea cliffs, cascading waterfalls, bamboo forests and green-winged macaws whose incessant screeches could well travel past the sound barrier. Akaka Falls was best accessible by foot trail and so we commenced walking down the natural pathways snaking down the lush tropical vegetation. Deeper into the rain forest, the fern grottos and bamboo trees imparted a unique sense of privacy. Continuing the trek, we saw palm trees growing out of lava rocks, ivy creepers covering ragged protrusions of rock formations, and colorful blooms of yellow, red and purple perennials. The towering bamboo forests stood as mute guardians of the verdant vegetation. I can't recall how far into the forest we had walked, when we decided to stop on a side trail for refreshments and a breather. More trekking eventually brought us in full view of the Akaka Falls—all 400 feet of it cascading in tiers, incessantly and unabatedly. Moments later, the guide nudged us into realizing that "gazing time" was over since we had a lot more ground to cover before heading back to the hotel. Further down, we stopped at the Rainbow Falls, which came down in a thundering descent and culminated in a pool that threw up foam and mist with equal force. Retracing our path to the parking lot we were relieved to be on the bus again, heading now to the Nani Mau Gardens—a world-class botanical site spanning over twenty acres. In Hawaiian language it meant "forever beautiful." On a guided tram ride tour across the length and breadth of the gardens, we explored acres of exotic tropical flowers sparkling with dewdrops. I do not recall their names or species but their vibrant hues stand out in my mind. There were bowers laden with hanging baskets of colorful begonias and fuchsias, rambling roses in shades of lavender, yellow, pink and black endowing the sidewalks with their fragrance and beauty, huge dahlias that dared you to grow them in your yard, delicate Himalayan blue poppies, and bright red "lehua" blossoms. Chugging past pools that were connected through architecturally inspired bridges, we stopped at a plant sanctuary to get a closer look at the ornamental plants: the orchid gardens where the multi-hued beauties seemed content to blaze their trail within their assigned territory, and Lady Giant Ferns in their lacey demeanor seemed to thrive on the beholden gaze of their admirers. The palm groves greeted visitors with tropical sophistication. There were large ornamental fan palms, fringed palms, date palms and many more from the palm family. To me, they were like abducted sentinels of the Hawaiian rain forests transported into civilization for furthering the cornucopia of horticulture.

As we boarded the flight back home from Hilo, part of me felt blessed to have been able to make this trip that brought about an awakening to a world out of sync, while the other part of me was saddened to leave behind a land, a culture and a people whose kindred spirit had enriched me and helped sustain memories everlasting.

The Certificate of Merit for Crossing the Equator, awarded to passengers on this cruise, appears on the following page:

CROSSING THE EQUATOR

Be it now proclaimed by Call of Conch and Nautilus throughout the Lattitudes and Longitudes of our Oceanic Domain that King Neptune, Ruler of the Seven Seas, King of the Secret Currents, Lord of the Boundless Waves, Master of the Tides, High Constable of the Coral Caverns and Uttermost Recesses of the Deep, do hereby Sanction and affirm that Our Most Noble Cross of the Equator be bestowed on ....*Theda Shatswat*.......... who but a mere Mortal, hath this 11th Day of October, 1998 on board Crown Princess accepted with Good Humor and Withstood with Fortitude a most Rigorous Initiation into the Ancient and Moistening Rites of our Aquatic Court.

In the Witness of

Alberto Guerrini
Captain

John Everett
Cruise Director

PRINCESS CRUISES
It's more than a cruise, it's the Love Boat.

Thirteen

Alpine Tour: Italy, Switzerland and Austria—August 1999

The Tahitian cruise was indeed a dream getaway where we had lost ourselves sauntering the charmed Polynesian Islands and observing the islanders' eclectic cultural mix of the ancient and the contemporary. The peaceful escapades away from the humdrum of everyday life helped recharge the soul and encourage an in-depth look at ourselves. This year around, we decided to focus on land tours to popular tourist resorts where few barriers existed between man and Nature's majesty.

Thus the summer of 1999 saw us vacationing in the Alpine regions of Italy, Switzerland and Austria. Three weeks of exploring the popular mountain resorts in this region etched in our minds indelible memories to last a lifetime.

Flying into Milan from the U.S. and driving by motor coach to Stressa, had us pretty exhausted by the end of the day. The Alpine ranges and picturesque little villages surrounded this premier Italian resort, situated on Lake Maggiore. History has it that the wealthy Piedmontese and Lombard families had invested in this area several centuries ago, building magnificent palaces and stately promenades. A short boat ride, next morning, took us to the Borromeo Isles once owned by Count Vitaliano. In the 1650s, he had transformed a barren island to the present Isola Bella. We walked through the exquisite terraced

150

gardens that showcased orange trees, cherry laurels, magnolias, camellias, sago palms and cedars. Continuing with the boat ride we visited the Fisherman Island, where small clustered homes lined narrow cobblestone alleys leading up to the village church. It was a fishing village in the 16th century and the small bell-tower of St. Vittore's church served as a lighthouse in the winter months for boats at sea.

The following day was a long drive to the sophisticated lakeside resort of Locarno in Switzerland. En route, we halted at Cannobio to sample the still prevalent world atmosphere of coffee houses where waitresses in white aprons and frilled caps waited on us with a smile. The most striking of all of Locarno's sites was the Franciscan Santuario della Madonna del Sasso Church, an impressive ochre vision on a wooded rock towering above the town. It was consecrated in 1487 on the spot where Virgin Mary was believed to have appeared to Brother Bartholomeo of the San Francesco Monastery. The walk up past the lush ravines and colorful stretches of wild flowers lasted a half-hour. The arcade of the church entrance extended a warm welcome to its faithful. The social buzz and public catwalk were concentrated in a square nearby, where fragrance seemed to waft from the lakeside gardens. Strolling down the alleys and stopping for an occasional drink was the tourists' way of blending in with Locarno life.

We headed back to Italy via rail, crossing the "One Hundred Valleys" past deep gorges, Alpine meadows and dense forests.

A day of relaxation followed and we were again on the go, more rested and rejuvenated this time around. We were in a ferry headed to Lake Orta—a sub alpine lake in the area. The lakefront homes were mansions in Baroque

151

and Romanesque styles. The decaying church in the alpine gorge, the slender waterfalls, the stillness in the air and the snow-capped mountains reaching out to the skies bring to mind Robert Browning's lines from "By the Fireside":

> *That speck of white just on its marge*
> *See Pella in the evening glow,*
> *How sharp the spearheads change*
> *When Alp meets Heaven in Snow!*

After a short stop at Isola San Giulio where a fortress from the 1600s is currently a convent for Benedictine nuns sworn to silence, we headed back home through the mountainous region of Mottarone, driving by the enormous towering statue of San Carlo Borromeo, the sixteenth century benefactor of the area.

A visit to Milan, the fashion capital of Europe, was one of the anticipated highlights of the trip. Commencing with a guided tour of the Art Museum at the Sforza Castele, we saw among other sculptures, Michaelangelo's last unfinished abstract masterpiece—The Pieta Rondanini. Our guide told us that it was charged with an emotion which only a trained eye could visualize. Very true, because I saw nothing that set my heart racing.

We then moved on to the Central Square and found ourselves facing one of the world's largest churches built in the 15th century, known as the Milan Duomo, second only to St. Peter's Basilica in Rome. Built in Gothic style, it is the seat of the Archbishop of Milan. It was an architectural marvel—the elaborately detailed gables, the angelic statues and the entire lofty creation in marble. Masters in creative writing probably do not endorse seeking refuge in famous quotations or dallying in others' erudition for a spark of inspiration. But I am really strapped for adequate rhetoric to describe this awe-inspiring structure and hence the following eloquent description by Mark Twain, the American writer, in his *Innocents Abroad*:

What a wonder it is! So grand, so solemn, so vast! And yet so delicate, so airy, so graceful. A very world of solid weight, and yet it seems—a delusion of frostwork that might vanish with a breath. Everywhere that a niche or perch can be found about the enormous building from summit to base, there is a marble statue and every statue a study in itself. Away, above, on the lofty roof rank on rank of carved and fretted spires spring high in the air, and through their rich tracery, one sees the sky beyond . . . They say that the Cathedral of Milan is second only to St. Peter's at Rome. I cannot understand how it can be second to anything made by human hands.

After an enjoyable lunch at the well known Via Napoleone, we were ushered into the Galleria Vittoro Emmanuele where the world's famous fashion designers display their latest creations. It was awesome to say the least, and we spent hours window-shopping for that was all we could afford. The eventful day thus came to a close.

Once again a day of leisure and we were on a nine hour transfer by motor coach to Switzerland. Through the Simplon Pass at an altitude of 7,500 feet, we entered the mountain village of Zermatt, nestling in a valley with the unmistakable Matterhorn looming large in the background. At first glance, it was obvious that there were no cars here nor were there luxury coaches busily letting off tourists and fumes at the same pace. Walking through the cobble streets of this quaint town past barns and chalets, we got a breathtaking view of the Matterhorn in all its glory and unsurpassed beauty. The refreshing camaraderie of the residents here knew no boundaries.

Gstaad, one of Switzerland's famous winter resorts in the Bernese Oberland of the Alps, was our next stop and an awaited one at that. We leisurely explored the charming one-street village, displaying wooden chalets and a solitary castle on the hilltop. It was a welcome change to see no autograph seekers here because it was an undisclosed destination of the celebrities.

Yet another night of rest and we were on the Belle Epoque Train to Montreux, the Queen of the Swiss Riviera, located on Lake Geneva. The morning was spent gazing and strolling past eighteenth-century stone houses with the typical ornate wrought-iron balconies. We later thronged around Charlie Chaplin's favorite haunt at Vevey for stills with the statue of the comedian.

I was in for an unbelievable surprise when the tour guide announced that we were now headed to the Castle of Chillon. I could not believe my ears. Was this the same castle that inspired Lord Byron to write his famous poem "Prisoner of Chillon"? My college years descended on me like an avalanche—the numerous hours that we spent in discussions of Byron's portrayal of Bonivard, the prisoner. Our brilliant but eccentric professor of English even made us enact the dramatic possibilities that might have crossed Bonivard's mind as he lay chained in the dungeon watching his fellow prisoners die one by one. Before long the Chateau was well within view. It was not as forbidding as I had pictured it to be, thanks to the Swiss penchant of hanging flower baskets to make entrances more inviting. This 13th-century castle outside Montreaux was the venue for Lord Byron's famous poem. Francois de Bonivard, the pivotal character, was a lay official at St.

Victor's Priory in Geneva who favored reformation and was hence shackled to a stone pillar by the Duke of Savoy in the 1530s. The castle, housing the chilling dungeons in its basement, was located on a rocky stretch in the waters with access to the mainland by a small bridge. Vaulted ceilings and ancient tapestries inside the castle seemed to bestow relief to the chateau's otherwise dreary interior. Ironic as it may seem, the dungeons have now become the focus of tourist attraction, thanks to Lord Byron who described them thus:

> *There are seven pillars of Gothic mould,*
> *In Chillon's dungeons deep and old,*
> *There are seven columns, massy and grey,*
> *Dim with a dull imprisoned ray,*
> *A sunbeam which hath lost its way;*
> *And thru the crevice and cleft*
> *Of the thick wall is fallen and left;*
> *Creeping o'er the floor so damp,*
> *Like a marsh's meteor lamp:*
> *And in each pillar there is a ring,*
> *And in each ring there is a chain,*
> *That iron is a cankering thing,*
> *For in these limbs its teeth remain,*
> *With marks that will not wear away*
> *Till I have done with this new day,*
> *Which now is painful to these eyes,*
> *Which have not seen the sun so rise,*
> *For years I cannot count them o'er,*
> *I lost their long and heavy score*
> *When my last brother droop'd and died,*
> *And I lay living by his side.*

Memories of the Castle of Chillon remained with me long after we left Montreaux—a process of unavoidable

The dungeons in the Castle of Chillon, where prisoner Bonivard was called "Prisoner of Chillon" by Lord Byron

rumination in an aging mind. The next day we were on the road again headed to Bernese Oberland, passing en route the huge lakes of Thun and Brienz. We paused to marvel at the thunderous Trummelbach Falls that came down with a rumble and roar defying the majesty of even the Niagara Falls.

At the glacier village of Grindelwald, we boarded the Jungfrau Rail Service to Kleine Scheidegg at an altitude of 7,000 feet, en route to Jungfraujoch atop the rugged Alpine mountains at 13,600 feet. I was awestruck at the sheer daringness of the concept. Running on meter guage with rack and pinion, the ride was one to remember. Taking in the spectacular panorama, savoring the unspoiled beauty of the mountainous landscape and watching the intermittent fog play an intimate game of hide and seek with the sunshine—the sights live on in my mind like happenings of yesterday. Tunneling through the Eiger Ranges, the increasingly steep incline of the rail-tracks seemed to preferentially hug the mountainside while we in turn hugged our seats in awe and fear, particularly while crossing bridges that spanned the gaping gorges. The intimate view of the triple peaks of Jungfrau, Eiger and Monch were at once so inspiring and yet so forbidding. They will remain as moments of a singular journey of epic beauty.

After an early breakfast next morning, we were on a nine-hour motor coach to Austria. Traveling past the Jungfrau ranges, we heaved sighs of relief each time the huge motor coach safely negotiated steep curves along the ravines and gorges. Undoubtedly we had paid for these spine-chilling experiences as well.

The golf town of Seefeld was our stopover for the night. At the crack of dawn, we were on the road again headed to Mittenwald—a picture perfect town in the Bavarian Alps where homes were decorated with traditional exterior frescoes. It had an ancient violin-making museum which connected to the deep history of classical music in this part of Europe. A traditional Tyrolean dinner in a log cabin, complete with wine and folk music, brought us full circle.

Next on the itinerary was a drive to Innsbruck, the capital of Tyrol. Medieval homes painted russet gray or pink still adorn the city as do the Tyrolean chalets. Continuing on to Salzburg, the birthplace of Mozart and the setting for the 1960s classic *Sound of Music,* this cultural center of Austria presented us an evening of classical music celebrating the legacy of the city's native prodigy Amadeus Mozart.

The Alpine tour was now coming to an end and the

concluding phase of the trip took us to the historic mountain village of Oberammergau. The Grimm's fairy tale houses reminiscent of Hansel and Gretel, and Red Riding Hood were positive tributes to the masterful wood carvings of the local Ettal monks.

We visited the royal Linderhoff Castle, done up in an unimaginably ornate fashion with golden bedrooms, hall of mirrors, a room service system whereby the dinner tables traveled to the kitchen and back at the press of a button, and very rightly earned the reigning king the title "Mad King Ludwig"!

It was time to bid adieu to our trip mates and exchange addresses. We then headed to Munich for our flight back to the U.S. On the highway, the motor coach slowed down to give us a fleeting glimpse of the unique BMW factory—a shimmering aluminum high rise with four towering cylinders set on an elevated rotunda. I only wished we had more time on our hands to do a detailed tour of this architectural icon—seemingly poised to project the ultimate in perfection. A comfortable flight brought us back to the warmth of our home and waiting family and friends.

Fourteen

Spain, Portugal and Morocco—August 2000

Our travels and journeys, by land and sea, had over time helped us amass a treasure trove of cherished memories—memories that stored the spirit and traditions of the countries we had visited, memories of amusing anecdotes on the trips (which were not as amusing when they occurred), and memories of endearing human connections. The irrefutable passion for getaway vacations had really come to stay.

This year, we decided to visit Spain, Portugal and Morocco where history has retained its own reflection through its rich heritage and unsullied traditions. Flamenco dancers, colorful carpets at the Souks, culinary delights, and a storied past of vibrant and enduring cultures were bound to make for a spectacular vacation. As always, we chose to go with tour companies for their time-tested expertise. The itineraries on escorted tours do remain structured in order to pack in more quality sight-seeing within an assigned time frame. One does sometimes get a feel of "scrambling for the school bus" days, but occasional stints of discipline even at this stage in life do not hurt.

On a pleasant mid-August evening in the year 2000, we boarded the overnight flight to Spain from an eastern gateway in the U.S. On arrival at the Barajas Airport in

Madrid, we were transferred to our hotel located in the heart of the bustling city. After a welcome drink with the tour director, we dispersed to our respective rooms, which compared very favorably with U.S. hotels. The liveried bellboys always sported a salute with a smile. The Spanish room service maids waited on us as though their lives depended on it—committed, polite and anxious to please even if they did not quite comprehend the English language. I noticed that one of them seemed to be following my lip movements very closely, leading me to believe that she was hard of hearing. So I went up close to her and spoke as loudly as I possibly could. Without annoyance or irritation and wearing the same serene smile, she indicated to me with gestures that she was not deaf but, *"No habla mucho Ingles"* (she did not speak much English). I realized at this point that the standard Spanish phrase I had memorized in the U.S. *"mucho gracias"* was not going to be adequate here. My husband's working knowledge of Spanish would be needed now more than ever. A short while later I called the concierge regarding hot and cold water problems in the shower. This time around, I spoke softly, clearly and deliberately. In less than five minutes a team arrived consisting of a plumber, an electrician, a room service tech. and a translator. The translator spoke more Spanglish than English and this time it was my turn to watch his lips!

Our room overlooked an immaculately maintained thoroughfare of Madrid. Stately trees lined the promenades in boulevard style. Expressways crisscrossed at heights with due deference to the skyline of the nation's capital. Automobiles whizzed past incessantly—I wondered if the rush hour in Madrid would ever end.

The "welcome dinner" that night at a traditional

Spanish restaurant enabled us to socialize with our traveling companions while our tour director listed the city's landmarks slated for sight-seeing next morning—the Royal Palace, the Plaza de la Cibeles in modern Madrid, and the Prado Museum, one of the greatest known art galleries in Europe. That evening we were to explore the city on our own and mingle with the fun loving and food loving Madrilenos whose pastime it was to frequent "tapas bars" and restaurants in the evening. The "La Cena" or typical Spanish dinner served that night, was a spread of salads, seafood, chicken, fried potatoes and specialty entrée. I enjoyed the "Arroz Cubano"—a mound of rice topped with tomato sauce and fried egg. It was different but delicious. Fresh fruit and flan (caramel custard) were served for dessert. Rioja wines, Spanish brandies, and Sangria were the choice of drinks available. Not much of a wine drinker myself, I did however relish the Sangria which was a blend of red wine, lemon, sliced orange and sugar. Life for the locals in Spain usually spruced up past 10 P.M. But we tourists had to call it a night in view of our itinerary next morning.

After an early breakfast of "bollas" (sweet rolls with jam) and Spanish coffee with hot frothy milk, we set out by motor coach to explore the lively Spanish capital located in the center of the Castillian plains. The Palacio de Oriente—the opulent Royal Palace—was an imposing structure situated in a garden setting which at one time was the site of the Hapsburgs' Alcazar. It did not function as an official residence of the Spanish monarchy but was used periodically for state events and celebrations. The majestic rooms inside this stately mansion catered to royal tastes. Their walls were covered with rich tapestries and crystal chandeliers hung from ornate ceilings adorned with frescoes and murals. An inscription on the cornerstone of the palace read "for all eternity." I pondered there for a few minutes wondering whether royalty thought they were playing "God" or was it a simple act of wishful thinking! Cherished collections of Spanish artwork by luminaries like Velazquez and El Greco were housed in different wings of the palace. Our guide, however, wished to move on to the "Throne Room," since we would anyway be viewing the magnificent paintings at our next stop—the Prado Museum. The Throne Room looked much like the "Durbar Halls" of the Indian Emperors. Ornate thrones sat on an elevation under a golden canopy. The walls were covered with crimson velvet, elaborate frescoes and shimmering chandeliers adorned the ceiling, and layers of carpeted steps led up to the throne. Two large bronze lions sat on either side "guarding" the approaches.

We stopped for lunch at one of the tapas bars. Tapas are a collection of large varieties of appetizers served with wine, making for a favorite mid-afternoon meal in Spanish circles. In the evening, the locals go hopping from bar to bar trying out different tapas. My husband and I had a field day with tortilla Espanola (Spanish omelette) and patatas bravas (potatoes with spicy sauce), considering that vegetarian options were limited in most countries. Torrijas (a type of French toast) was one of the many pastries I relished. While the men folk indulged in Spain's coveted wine "sherry," I opted for the steaming delicious Spanish hot chocolate.

Refreshed and rejuvenated, we headed to the Museo Prado—one of Madrid's premier attractions. It was a large terra cotta building conceived in neoclassical style, sporting six massive pillars holding the super structure in sculptured relief. In response to our questions on the term "neoclassical," the guide apologized for his lack of erudition in defining architectural terms in English and managed to explain it away as "Bordering on Tradition with a touch of Bourbon." I personally didn't get it and neither did the others! The Prado is the monumental pride of Spain and one of Europe's largest museums carrying the world's coveted collections of art. It stands as a glowing tribute to centuries of dedication of the Spanish royalty and art collectors alike. Since we did not have time to cover the museum in its entirety, our guide walked us through some of the treasures of Prado Museum, which included masterpieces by Velasquez, Goya and Murillo. I was all ears trying to objectively glean the guide's explanations as we paused to view the paintings firsthand. But before long I found myself writing down merely the names of the artists and their works, unable to follow his incomprehensible terminologies in Spanglish!

Velasquez: Lived in Madrid as a court painter to King Phillip IV. A very skilled artist of his times, he blended color, light and space for effect. Two of his outstanding works were: "The Surrender of Breda," an equestrian portrait of King Phillip IV, and "The Maids of Honor," which to me was essentially a portrait of the royal family of 1656 with artist Velasquez in it as well. Apparently it was different in that the lavish strokes of the painter's brush focused more on the maids-in-waiting and hence the title.

Goya: Brilliant in the depiction of the aristocracy of his time. "Third of May" was his vivid painting of a firing squad during the War of Independence. It grimly reflected the senseless brutality that unquestioned power could inflict.

Murillo: Excelled in portraying infant themes. "The Good Shepherd" depicts an inner peace and serenity beautifully reflected on a child's face while he caressed a lamb. "Virgin with a Rosary" detailed a child's comfort and sense of security on the lap of a mother figure. "The Immaculate Concept of Soult" showed the Virgin surrounded by little angels whose faces were pictures of heavenly innocence. This painting was apparently confiscated by Napoleon's General "Soult" and later returned to Museo Prado. Hence the caption. Most of the collections in the museum were works dating from 19th century and earlier.

We briefly halted at Centro de Arte Reina Sofia for a quick glance of Picasso's monumental work "Guernica" displayed under bulletproof glass. It was a spine-chilling depiction of the massacre, which took place in the small village of Guernica during the Spanish Civil War. In fifteen minutes, we were herded back to continue with the panoramic city tour covering Plaza De La Cibeles in modern Madrid—a rotunda of floodlit fountains, manicured grounds and historic buildings. Proceeding to the old quarter, which was a favorite joint for the local Spanish and tourists alike, the Plaza Mayor was packed with cafes and bars accounting for the buzz and humdrum in the area.

Back to the hotel for an evening on our own, many of our companions opted for the Bull Ring at Las Ventas to watch a bull fight. It was an integral part of Spanish culture, they said, and the tour would be incomplete without witnessing it. Nothing or nobody was going to convince me to sit through those gory sights. My husband and I decided to stroll down the tree-lined avenues of this cosmopolitan capital, and stopping at the tapas bars for a bite to eat while indulging in "people watching" as they sipped an aperitif before dinner.

As evening set in, steady streams of home bound office goers whizzed past us, some on foot, some on bikes and others getting on and off the bus. At a street corner, we saw a musician in tattered clothes strumming on his guitar seated on a three-legged metal stool which was rusted from use and exposure to the elements. His face was lean and gaunt, his expressive deep brown eyes sunken in their sockets, and his graying hair disheveled on a balding head. He was, however, a picture of concentration as he serenaded his audience with "Santa Lucia." An old canvas hat sat on the dusty ground across from him for those who wanted to donate a coin or two. In the normal course, I might have walked past him depositing a few pesos in his hat. But the eloquent rendering of the familiar song made me stop in my track. In a fleeting instant, I was back to my high school music class where "Santa Lucia" was sung and played ever so often. We lingered on to hear the guitarist. Lowly by birth or fate, this man seemed to have a tremendous sense of pride in his talent regardless of where or how it was displayed. My allergic coughs as I stood there might have disturbed his concentration now and again but he did not let on any evidence of that.

At the end of the evening when the audience began to disperse, I threw in my donation before moving on. He saw that and gestured for us to wait. I watched him delve into his creaky old trunk and take out a corked bluish-green square bottle containing some oily fluid. He walked toward me, his demeanor still a picture of concentration and said, "Senora, this is for you."

Without taking my eyes off that greasy bottle, I asked him, "What is it?"

He replied, "Fish oil. Good for your asthma." Before I could refute his established diagnosis, my husband politely explained to him that since we were tourists and constantly on the go, it would be difficult for us to carry that bottle along. The man reverently made a sign of the cross and said, *"Yo probe, solo los Dios pueden ayudarte,"* meaning "I tried; only God can help you."

We respectfully bowed and continued walking. This nameless and homeless individual surfaced in our thoughts for the rest of the evening. He had a heart larger than his physique and a soul twice blessed by the Lord. We stopped at a local restaurant for dinner. Unsure of the names of dishes that were totally vegetarian, we ordered "cocido madrileno," which was essentially a stew of chick peas, cabbage, turnips, carrots and potatoes. We had requested it without chicken or beef when the waitress quipped: "You want pork, I see." I categorically told her that we did not eat meat or pork for religious reasons. The word "religious" seemed to convey it all to her. We indulged in the flan (caramel custard as we call it here) and Spanish coffee, before calling it a day. While walking back to our hotel all we could talk about was the unpretentious guitarist and his message of universal caring—the kind that exists beyond the confines of manors or hutments.

The following morning we were headed to medieval Toledo, once known as the "City of Three Cultures" for the harmonious co-existence of Christian, Muslim and Jewish communities here. Sadly, such a concept does not exist in the annals of civilized living today. En route, we drove through the province of Cuidad to Alcazarde San Juan. The purpose of this stopover was to view the statues of Don Quixote and his faithful squire Sancho Panza standing side by side in the city plaza. We learned that these characters, from a novel written by Cervantes, had come to be regarded as iconic images in Spain. Don Quixote, an illusion-struck commoner of La Mancha, was portrayed as fantasizing to be a knight in armor and with his equally delusional squire Sancho Panza, he set out to seek his imaginary ladylove. En route he saw the wayside windmills as likely approaching enemies that needed to be conquered! After several such episodes outside the realm of reality, the novel characterizes him as finally having regained sanity and normalcy. The spindly figure of Don Quixote on his aging pony and pot-bellied Sancho Panza on the donkey set all our cameras flashing and we carried back on film these notable characters in Spanish literature.

Toledo was an hour's drive from La Mancha. The approach to this hilltop town overlooking the Tagus River, abounded in towers, ancient gateways and palatial structures built in predominantly Moorish style, "Moorish" being the Spaniards' version of the word "Muslim." Narrow streets wound past historic Gothic buildings and cathedrals. With only a few hours allotted for sightseeing in Toledo, we first visited El Alcazar, a 16th-century Moorish citadel that stood out as a towering edifice. The museum inside had carried an impressive display of war memorabilia dedicated to the fallen heroes of the Spanish Civil War. We then headed to the city's most famous synagogue—Santa Maria la Blanca. Constructed in the 1200s on Christian territory by Moorish architects for Jewish use, this great monument of religious harmony was different with its stark white walls and brick pillars carrying horseshoe-shaped arches. It was typical Almohad architecture, we were told. It became a church in the 15th century and continues to be known as Santa Maria la Blanca (Saint Mary, the White). Our final stop at Toledo was the Church of Santo Tome—originally a mosque and rebuilt as a Gothic church in the 14th century. Located in the vicinity of artist El Greco's residence, his famous work "The Burial of Count of Orgaz" drew a constant stream of visitors. Painted around 1588, it portrayed the miracle that occurred at the time of the burial of the count—that of St. Augustine and St. Stephen descended from heaven to help lower the body in the tomb. Interestingly, the mourners in the painting are depicted as contemporaries of El Greco. We stopped for a quick lunch before continuing our motor coach ride into Andalusia to Moorish hilltop Granada while all of Spain observed "siesta hour" between 2 and 4 P.M.

Granada at the foot of the spectacular Sierra Nevada's snow covered mountains was founded by the Moors in the 8th century. Outside the city's boundaries the terrain was sandy and desolate. The narrow winding streets of the Moorish quarters dated back to the times before the advent of motor vehicles. The Gothic chapel and Renaissance cathedral existed in peaceful harmony with exquisite Islamic architecture indicating the civility of the times. We were settled into a charming, recently restored holiday home and following an early dinner of complimentary tapas, we retired for a good night's rest.

The next morning was the eagerly anticipated visit to the exquisite Alhambra Palace, the bastion of Muslim architectural glory and the former residence of Moorish rulers. We were urged to attend an hour-long orientation on the history and architecture of this icon which has been glorified in tales and sung in ballads. The lecture hour commenced with the opening lines: *"Si has muerto sin ver la Alhambra no has vivido"* (meaning if you have died without seeing the Alhambra, you have not lived).

Alhambra in Arabic meaning "crimson castle" was apparently conceived by the Nasrite emirs in the mid-1200s to encompass an "alcazaba" (fortress), an "alcazar" (palace) and a "medina" (city) all rolled in one. Enduring the changing faces of history and conquests, the Alhambra came under Christian rule in 1492 with the advent of King Ferdinand's monarchy. Emperor Charles V in the 1500s left his imprint by modifying some of the architectural details in Renaissance style, creating thereby an out of sync appearance within the palace complex. By the 1800s, the glorious Moorish architecture was in danger of being further defaced when help came in the form of restoration and preservation by Ferdinand VII in 1870. To this day it continues to be a national monument and a venerated tourist attraction in Spain.

The Alhambra consisted of three sections:

1. The Royal Palace (which would be the focus of our visit) complete with the Mexuar, the Serallo and the Harem housing the popular Lion's Court.
2. The Gardens of Generalife preserved in Moorish fashion with fountains, cypress avenues and grottos.
3. The Fortress of Alcazaba where the watchtower and a turret with a huge bell, were situated.

We were adequately briefed on Alhambra history as we set out to visit this fabled palace of the Moors. The entrance to the Palacio Arabe was through a small door from where a corridor led us to a huge courtyard. In the center was a large pond flanked by myrtles. From here, we were shown into the Hall of Ambassadors. It was an ornate reception area, perfectly square in shape with the sultan's throne facing the entrance. There were numerous arched windows in traditional Islamic style, an intricately decorated ceiling in white gold and blue with a dome depicting the "seven heavens," and stucco walls detailed with Moorish filigree designs. The room had the welcome look needed to entertain dignitaries in that culture. It was here that the reigning sultan signed Granada's surrender to King Fernando. This was the Serallo that came into existence in the 14th century. Most of the palace rooms were quadrangular with ceilings painted in red, gold and blue and supported by marble pillars fanning out into arches. The paneling on the walls had painted tiles with arabesque motifs. Most of the rooms opened on to a central courtyard bordered by arcaded hallways and this pattern repeated itself throughout the palace.

The Mexuar was the section of the Royal Palace where the sultans conducted business. It was on the same lines as the other areas but a lot more subdued in décor. We were then escorted to the celebrated "Court of the Lions"—a huge rectangular area paved with richly colored tiles and bordered with elaborately designed pillars. In the center of the courtyard was the 12-sided marble "Fountain of Lions." A large alabaster basin sat on the backs of the lions directing water into their mouths, which in turn formed spouts to flow into the encircling waterway. The lions court led into three celebrated areas—the Hall of the Two Sisters so named because of the twin flawless marble slabs in the pavement, the Hall of the Abencerrages where the father of the last King of Granada massacred invited chiefs at a banquet here, and the Hall of the Kings of which jointly constituted the Harem.

The arena shot into prominence when America's literary celebrity Washington Irving romanticized it in his book *The Tales of Alhambra* in 1832. Inspired by the grandeur of the Moorish setting during his stay at the Palace in 1829, he had this to say about the "Lions Court": "It is impossible to contemplate this scene, so perfectly Oriental, without feeling the early associations of Arabian romance, and almost expecting to see the white arm of some mysterious princess beckoning from the gallery or some dark eye sparkling through the lattice. The abode of beauty is here as if it had been inhabited but yesterday."

We bid goodbye to this legendary pride of Moorish architecture, and headed to a nearby restaurant for lunch—a choice of garlic soup, potato omelet, rabbit stew, salads and fresh fruit served with wine.

We were on the road again continuing on Spain's Mediterranean coast to Costa del Sol (the Sunshine Coast) in the nearby province of Malaga. Clean and sandy beaches extended for miles, with an abundance of palm and cypress trees alongside. Bougainvillea bowers graced the sweeping terraces and roof gardens of the white-washed Spanish villas. The locals in tiny fishing villages waved us flying kisses as we drove by. The appeal of the Mediterranean landscape and culture of this region was addicting. Torremolinos, a Costa del Sol resort, was our stopover for the night. We were accommodated in a comfortable holiday villa situated across the seaside promenade. The sun-bathers in this classic Andalusian region were still on the sands, wind surfers and water skiers indulged in their aquatic pleasures, while tourists with no specific agenda frequented the sea-front restaurants for barbecued sardines and fried fish. My husband and I took a horse drawn coach ride through the narrow cobbled streets with the gentle balmy breeze brushing against us. We watched life unfold in this charming coastal resort. I saw no guitarist or street performers here that night—this was a playing field for the rich and the famous. Upscale stores displayed Lladro figurines, Damascene jewelry, ceramics and silver. Local markets (baratillos) competed for the few likely bargain hunters among the wealthy and the opulent. We were constantly alerted to beware of pickpockets and, as a result, dinnertime in a busy Spanish restaurant was spent watching our wallets rather than relishing the cuisine.

The next morning, we were on the coach again driving to Algeciras for the transit into Morocco. In this noisy port town, we boarded a ferry for the half-hour crossing across the Strait of Gibraltar to exotic Morocco. We continued past the Rif Mountains, the cedar forests and narrow gorges as we headed to the imperial city of Fez for a two-day stay. The largest city of the medieval world, Fez was founded in 789 A.D. and served as capital of Morocco for 400 years. Our hotel, situated in the heart of the city, was an authentic Moorish "riad"—a majestic Moroccan guesthouse built around a courtyard. The entrance was imposing with marbled columns and detailed arches. As we walked into the dazzling foyer, turbaned bellboys brought around trays of dried fruits and fresh juice, according us a welcome in "sultan style." We felt this way not because of any delusions of grandeur but from the lavishness of the ambience. Our ornately furnished rooms opened into spacious, terraced sit-outs overlooking the fabulous gardens. Buffet lunch was served in the banquet hall, the spread consisting of a choice of couscous (semolina grains) and tajines—stew with meat, potatoes and vegetables. There were chicken dishes roasted with olives and whole lamb spitted over an open fire. The vegetarians were treated to a Moroccan salad made with tomatoes, cucumbers and onions, harira—a spicy chickpea based soup, roasted peppers and eggplant babaganouj. Pastries stuffed with honeyed ground almonds reminded me of the baklavas in the U.S.

We set out in taxis braving the sweltering heat outside and were offloaded at the gates of the medina, which was a strictly car-free zone. We carried bottled water hoping that frequent sips would keep us hydrated through the afternoon. The Moroccan medina, which separated Old Fez (Fez el Bali) from the New Fez (Fez el Djedid), abounded in domes and minarets, mosques and madrassas (Islamic religious schools) and numerous shops and wayside food stalls. Arabic was the prime spoken language with French being a close second.

As we walked past the city walls, hustlers aggressively competed for our attention, but our hotel appointed guide did a superb job of keeping them at bay. Most of the time the guide walked ahead looking away as he spoke, which gave me the feeling that eye contact with women could possibly be a cardinal sin in this country. The new Fez city, he said, was home to royal palaces, monuments and exquisite gardens, while the French constructed the Ville Nouvelle with bars and café joints to make it more appealing to tourists. We walked down the dusty narrow streets of the labyrinthine medina which were lined with improvised stores brimming with wares. We saw bearded artisans hammering away sheets of brass and copper, spice markets with wafting aromas of ginger, cumin, pepper and saffron, and souks displaying a variety of Moroccan handicrafts. The pottery predominated over all else with bowls, plates, vases and jugs in a medley of white and blue designs, chunky silver jewelry set with amber stones, and painstakingly carved woodwork. The stench of the open sewers alongside had to be contended with, but that did not deter me from stopping to browse at the souvenir stalls. Our guide had apprised us of the accepted practice of prospective buyers keeping the shopkeepers in good humor through the ups and downs of bargaining and once a deal was struck, it was meant to be honored. Language was no barrier and with some negotiations, I settled for a few blue and white ceramic teapots inlaid with silver. Just about then we heard a loud announcement in Arabic and we assumed it to be the amplified call of the "muezzins" (crier) to prayer. But surprisingly, we saw no such intent. The crowds moved to the sides, making way for somebody or something to pass by. Before long a few donkeys heavily laden with goods lazily sauntered along in single file. Donkeys did have the right of way in this country! In all our travels, we had never encountered this form of observed regimentation for beasts of burden.

In the heart of the medina was the enormous marble Kairaouine Mosque founded in the 9th century. Non-Moslems were not allowed entry into Moroccan mosques. However we got a glimpse of the medieval architecture adorning the mighty doors, the fountains and the courtyards. Situated across the road was a popular Quranic school carved in cedar and stucco. The scorching sun overhead, the seemingly unquenchable thirst, and rivulets of incessant sweat on our torsos made us want to return to the air-conditioned comfort of our hotel. As we headed back in a "Petit" cab, the guide educated us on the terminologies associated with the holy mosque. "Masjid," he said, represented the venue of prostration and the "Quiblah" oriented towards Kabah in Mecca contained the prayer niche. Islam's directive forbidding idolatry resulted in all the decorations taking geometric shapes and calligraphic inscriptions from the Quran. Near the mosque was the shrine of Moulay Idris II where believers congregated for miracles—the deformed in the hope of being made whole, the faithful steeped in prayer and yet others lay prostrated hoping for an intercession by the saint. Women shrouded in traditional gowns stopped at wayside stalls for lotions and potions, for jasmines and fragrances and kohl and cinnamon scrubs. Clearly Fez was content to remain steeped in tradition in spite of existing in a rapidly advancing world.

Back in the confines of our hotel room we were rested and refreshed before setting out later in the evening to an ancient palace hotel for an authentic feast and live Moroccan belly dancing. No dress codes were enforced here but as always I indulged in wearing my Indian sari, this time in black and gold silk. The restaurant was done up in Moroccan décor. Seating was on low couches or on colorful plush carpets with large woven pillows. Crystal chandeliers shimmered overhead as we seated ourselves closest to the dance floor in the center of the room. The audience was a mix of tourists and locals—a crowd of warm, hospitable and ethnically tolerant people. The Moroccan meal was served before the mesmerizing belly dancer was due to make her appearance. Freshly baked bread was the common all-purpose dish at each table. The Maghreb salad, Algerian green beans, the harira (lentil soup), and the pastilla (pigeon pie with almonds) which also came as a vegetarian dish constituted the cuisine for the evening. Honeyed pastries and sweet mint tea followed. The lilting Middle-Eastern music in the background reminded me of the strains of "shehnai" played during celebrated events in India.

Before long, in a flashing dazzle the belly dancer made her appearance. She was an epitome of beauty, dressed in a sequin-studded turquoise silk skirt, which precariously clung to her shapely hips below the navel, a glittering bra for added focus to her contour and a beaded turquoise head band which kept her highlighted brown hair in place. Adorning her slender neck, and her delicate wrists, were several strands of traditional jewelry—enough to showcase all of Moroccan art. Sparkling earrings cascaded down to her shoulders. Henna designs in mehendi style covered her hands and feet while a gossamer-thin turquoise scarf hung loosely around her neck. She swayed slowly from side to side as she walked toward the guests. Her gaze, unfortunately, settled on our table. My heart froze as she came up to me with a beaming smile and looking me straight in the eye, threw her gossamer scarf around me. In belly dancing parlance, it meant that she was beckoning me to the dance floor. I entreatingly looked around for help—somebody, anybody, to get me out of this predicament. My amused husband, grinning from ear to ear, goaded me to do her bidding. "Be a sport," he said.

As in a trance, I reluctantly rose from my seat. My lips were parched, my throat was dry and my limbs were heavy as lead. I managed to carry my benumbed torso to the dance floor, oblivious to the gazes and smirks of the amused onlookers. Once there, the belly dancer positioned me across from her, fitted finger cymbals on both of us and gestured me to follow her moves as best as I could. My hearing and vision were probably the only cognitary senses that were still functional at the time. The sensual rhythmic dance commenced with slow undulating moves. Her hips moved in a circle while she threw constant glances at me to supervise my participation. I shuffled my feet from side to side hoping that it would render a semblance of some hip swaying. Her transitions from one movement to another were happening so fast that I could hardly keep up. Her arms were already up in the air in a wide sweeping gait while her hands glided in rippling moves much like a serpent. Even as I hastened to get to these which seemed more doable, I found that my feet had come to a standstill. There was no way I could keep up with these nuances of execution. The belly dancer had progressed into stomach flutters and continuous spins while all I could feel was a spin inside my head. Regardless, I continued with a few arm and leg moves. After what seemed an eternity, the dancer slowed down, patted me on the shoulder and escorted me back to my seat amidst standing ovation from the packed house. It was time now to put the past behind and regain my composure. Having to belly dance in my mid-fifties to a full house in a strange country was no picnic by any stretch of imagination. Back in the hotel that night, I slept like a baby after all the mental rigors of the evening. One determination I had made at the end of the day was, no more wearing the sari as long as I was in Morocco. It was very possible that the loose skirt-like appearance of my sari wrapped around the lower torso much like the belly dancer's, might have induced her to consider me a likely target for a dance partner.

In spite of my achy knees and hands, I joined the tour group next morning for the scheduled sightseeing. On the itinerary were visits to the city's landmarks, the tanneries and the Moroccan carpet factory. A Moroccan carpet was the one everlasting souvenir that my husband and I had decided to acquire on this trip. Hence all my aches and pains had to be kept at bay till the carpet selection was made.

The Royal Palace was off limits for tourists but we got to have a glance of its large brass doors that were bordered with intricate mosaic carvings. The rooms were done up in standard palace décor and pillars inlaid with marble graced the patios. The sultan's espouse room was insulated from heat and noise for obvious reasons. The Bab Boujeloud Gate was a famed archway, which marked the end of the New Fez and the beginning of the Old Fez. We paused at the entrance to admire the workmanship of the artisans in transitioning the mosaic decor from blue (the city color of Fez) to green (the color of Islam) with fluidity and grace. We then walked to the nearby Dar Batha Museum gardens for a quick lunch in the cool shade of the century-old sprawling trees. At this point, our guide ran by us two options for the afternoon:

1. A visit to the tanneries for those interested in watching the process of tanning. From adjoining terraces one could have a great view of the dyeing pits filled with pigeon excrements and fermented chaff, vats carrying saffron yellow, poppy red and indigo blue dyes, and bare chested men bathed in perspiration eking out a livelihood stretching goat and camel hides.

Or

2. A visit to a reputed Moroccan carpet showroom and the adjoining looms for a firsthand view of carpet weaving.

Without hesitation, we opted for the latter choice. In the company of our trustworthy and knowledgeable hotel guide, we were shuttled to the renowned house of carpets. A brief orientation en route taught us that the quality of threads and number of knots in a carpet would be the prime factors in deciding the price. Bargaining was imperative and starting at a fifth of the quoted price was the acceptable norm. Under no circumstance should one settle for more than half the asking price. The showroom was an old three-storied building with no elevators or air-conditioning. Carpets were displayed on the walls, some were laid out on the floors and others graced the entranceway. Only foreigners were allowed access to exclusive carpets, without prior appointments. Ceiling fans droned overhead and trays of fresh fruit juice were brought around with young boys fanning away the flies—a special service for foreign customers, we were told. There were woolen carpets, silk carpets and cotton carpets in darker shades and pastel hues woven by the nomadic Berbers. The motifs, however, were limited to rectilinear, grids, diamond-shaped or stripes. Adherence to these designated designs make Moroccan carpets distinctly different from most others. After hours of sweating it out physically and rhetorically, we settled for a living room rug in shades of aqua and burnt orange. The final price was haggled down to 50 percent of the quoted figure but this did not include tips, shipping, insurance and duty. Our ultimate payment magically totaled back to the original asking price! A short stopover at the adjoining factory enabled us see the shanty rooms that were hotter than saunas where little girls busily worked at looms that were suspended from the ceilings. Their tiny nimble fingers deftly moved in and around the weave to produce the desired patterns. Child labor we were told was in great demand in view of the "little fingers."

The next morning an exciting drive took us through the foothills of the Atlas Mountains to Marrakesh, Africa's most popular all-season resort. It was at one time known to be the favorite holiday spot of Sir Winston Churchill. Our motor coach wound its way through cedar forested hills, across narrow gorges, and past tiny villages dotted with mud homes and emaciated camels. It was hair-raising to see improvised stalls perched along the cliff edges, peddling pottery and beaded jewelry. A view of this terracotta clad imperial city from the mountain elevations was tantamount to dipping into timeless enchantment. Verdant date palm trees silhouetted against the blazing sun, terraced fields of wheat swaying in the gentle breeze, a galaxy of mosques, palaces and gardens that heritage had called its own, and the modern villas luxuriously laid out to remain relevant in the contemporary world, were real manifestations of surreal beauty. Our hotel here was a refurbished palace located in close proximity to the city's landmarks. Brick and marble archways lining the mosaic corridors, cathedral ceilings, marbled baths, ancient paintings and rooms furnished with the trappings of the sultans, gave us the ultimate in comfort. Moroccan cuisine was very similar except that this hotel served an added specialty called "tangia"—a dish of meat and spices stewed overnight over glowing embers. The strong aroma of the Moroccan coffee here was irresistible even to the casual coffee drinker as were the gourmet almonds, dates and pastries.

In the afternoon, while the muezzin called the faithful to prayer, a few of us decided to take a leisurely stroll of the neighborhood. The souks displayed colorful kaftans, prayer carpets, and souvenir stores like the ones we had seen in Fez. Camels chewed lazily on their cud with froth lining their cavernous mouths as they stood for a breather before being whipped back into action. Fortune tellers predicted the impossible, men with performing monkeys relentlessly continued with their shows, and snake charmers with boas around their neck and slithering reptiles in wicker baskets competed for attention. Magicians manifested white doves out of nowhere and acrobats pole-vaulted to rollover in mid-air. Friendly locals stopped to greet us with "Salaam Aleikum" meaning "peace be with you." We smiled and nodded not knowing how to quite reciprocate the sentiment. I had a gnawing concern that we might have looked like a bunch of disturbed individuals, thereby prompting that form of greeting. But I later learned that it was a commonly used form of salutation in Islamic culture. For dinner that night at the hotel, we had a spread of eggplant casserole with cheese, sweet and sour artichokes, spinach and potato pie and couscous. The next morning we were slated to visit the Djemma el Fna Square, the Bahia Palace and view the Koutoubia Mosque.

The Bahia Palace, a 19th-century harem, was commissioned by Si Ahmed Ben Musa, a former black slave who over the years rose to power and wealth. Even through the ravages of time, its layout unmistakably conveyed a sense of its erstwhile beauty. As with all Moroccan palaces, the rooms overlooked a sprawling courtyard with a central fountain. The décor of each room catered to the whims of the many wives and concubines. Located on extensive grounds, the ceramic tiled walls, ceilings inlaid with marble, and symmetric arches represented the architecture of yesteryears. We were to spend the rest of the day at the famous Djemma el Fna Square known to bustle with life from daybreak to sundown. With no guide assigned to us at this time, we guarded our handbags and wallets as we commenced to amble through the winding streets making our way through a sea of humanity. Wayside singers performed in gay abandon, healers and mendicants reached out to the gullible, and fruit stalls loaded with tangerines, lemons and grapes were the focus of foreigners who were not brave enough to sample local delicacies. The food stalls were geared to serve delectable dishes on short order. Language was not an issue since one just had to gesture to what they wanted. The rule of thumb for visiting foreigners was to follow the local Moroccans to the eateries in order to be assured of the best cuisine. We did just that and found ourselves indulging in lip-smacking eggplant dishes—baked eggplant, minted eggplant with lemon and garlic, and eggplant tomato salad served with flat bread.

Continuing our trek through the dusty lanes, we walked past souks displaying filigreed brassware and hanging lamps, improvised stalls with mounds of figs, olives, nuts and dates, poultry enclosures where live pigeons and turkeys cackled as they nervously looked around, carpet souks in a medley of colors and indigenous designs and leather souks that had posted aggressive salesmen to bring in customers who so much as even glanced at any of the assorted Moroccan leather goods. The souvenir stalls here sported a wider variety of wares and for those of us with a penchant for collecting artifacts, the exquisitely engraved silver jewelry boxes studded with semi-precious stones were a must. "Salaam Aleikum," I said to the pretty lady who stood there garbed in the traditional "selham" and a scarf covering her head instead of the mandated veil. Her large dark eyes took me in while a faint smile adorned her petal-pink lips. She greeted me in reciprocation and asked me in fluent English which of the souvenirs I fancied. She went on to say that her family lived in England and that she was on vacation here filling in for a friend. I cherished those kindred moments in a foreign land even as I waited for the souvenirs to be wrapped. I could not get myself to haggle with her on the prices but she gave me a good discount on her own.

We drove by the red-stoned Mosque of Koutoubia which the Moroccans hold in utmost spiritual veneration. It had been in existence from the 12th century towering above the city's marketplace. It was from here that the muezzins proclaimed the call to worship five times a day. On our way back to the hotel we drove by the 30-foot-high ochre city gates. Waiting horse carriages transported tourists to entrances of their choice and the coachmen graciously acknowledged a generous tip with a "salaam" (salute).

Bidding goodbye to Marrakesh, we were headed next morning on a 4-hour drive to Casablanca for a day's stay in the nation's largest city. The prime tourist attraction here was the Mosque of Hassan II completed in 1993. The second largest mosque in the world and one of the few Moroccan mosques that allowed entry to non-Moslems, it was designed by a French architect at a cost of several million dollars. It is a monumental tribute to Moorish architecture and an inspiring interface of the old and the new. Situated on the waters of the North Atlantic Ocean, its 700 feet minaret is the tallest in the world. Andalusian influence dominated the intricate workmanship of the blue and white minaret, which by night directs laser beams towards Mecca.

Approach to the mosque was across a huge tiled courtyard. The gleaming beige marble exterior with intricately carved walls and columns that supported horseshoe arches were a study in design and beauty. First-time visitors like us were awe-struck at the dedicated elegance of this edifice. Prior to entering the holy place for a guided tour, we had to remove our shoes, cover our heads and follow the biddings of the guide. I had never entered a mosque before and did not quite know what to expect. There were no idols or pictures nor were there altars or sanctum sanctorums. The enormity of the hall, the large white granite columns on spotless marble floors, the prayer area carpeted in red and the dazzling chandeliers overhead left us speechless. There was no segregation between rich and poor for every believer was created equal. The women's gallery on the upper level was carved in dark wood and marble fountains and community baths were situated in the lower level of the mosque. During the course of the forty-minute guided tour, we learned that this mosque was built to withstand earthquakes and equipped with heated floors, electric doors and sliding roofs that opened up for a symbolic direct view of Heaven. Part of the mosque's floor, we were told, was made of glass for worshippers to kneel over the sea. It was, however, out of bounds for visitors. Exiting this ornate yet spartan house of worship, I was once again reminded of Mark Twain's words: *"What a wonder it is! So grand, so solemn, so vast. And yet so delicate, so airy, so graceful."*

As we stepped out into the real world of this Arab metropolis, I was intrigued by the sight of innumerable men in colorful outfits and large hats, making a trade of selling cups of water from polished copper pitchers. Anything to earn a few honest bucks, I realized. With the mercury soaring sky high at noontime, this probably was the most patronized service on the streets at that hour. An older Moroccan man dressed in traditional "kurta" and "pyjama" stopped to talk to one of our Caucasian trip mates. He conversed in fluent English and some of us gathered to hear him. He reminisced about the famous movie *Casablanca* filmed in Hollywood in 1942. Even to this day, he said, the romance of the lead artistes Humphrey Bogart and Ingrid Bergman in the movie made hearts flutter in this namesake town a world away. Later in the day, some of our friends made a hurried dash to the casbah to pick up last minute souvenirs while we decided to relax in our hotel room. Having negotiated the streets and alleys of one casbah, we knew what all casbahs were likely to be.

Next day we were headed to the Moroccan capital Rabat, en route to Tangier. We were assigned three hours of sight-seeing time at the royal mosque, the Mausoleum and the royal palace. As we drove through the gleaming white city, the towering date palms joined in with the clear blue skies and the ravishing ocean waters to accord us an enchantingly scenic welcome.

The marble mausoleum was no less a masterpiece than other edifices of Moorish grandeur. The arch-shaped entrance was ensconced in trellised marble carvings, with a tiled green pyramid rising above the roof in archaic splendor. Inside the mausoleum was a raised rectangular onyx platform that entombed King Hassan II's coffin. Across from the mausoleum was the Hassan mosque. Its minaret was one of the country's icons and differed from most others in that each of its faces carried a varying architectural relief. The royal palace was a sprawling classic constructed in keeping with tradition. It was laid out amidst sunken gardens that were designed to provide continuous bursts of color and fragrance.

Before heading out to Tangier for the night's stay, we were treated to Moorish coffee and "gazelle horns" (a Moroccan cake) as a memento of our brief visit to the capital city. On the road again, we were apprised of our options for the afternoon:

1. Exploring Tangier on our own which basically

comprised visits to the casbahs and medinas, the Catholic Church that sat alongside the largest Mosque of the city, and the Tangier American Legation Museum where one could see interesting artifacts donated by the late Malcolm Forbes.

2. A drive to Cape Spartel, eight miles from Tangier where the Atlantic Ocean and the Mediterranean Sea met. The tour guide constantly reminded us of the importance of the term "La Shukran" (meaning No, Thank You) to fend off aggressive vendors who had the propensity to hound tourists for the entire duration of their visit.

Having offloaded some of our companions and all of our luggage at Tangier, we proceeded to Cape Spartel, a beautiful resort town located in a lush, verdant setting across the sea. On the sands around the lighthouse, flowering cacti made their random appearance amidst ancient rock formations while palm fronds swayed with the gentle sea breeze. Enterprising tourists lined up for camel rides on the beach which were being offered for a bargain price of a buck a person. Camels festively decorated with multi-colored pompoms in yellow, pink, orange, blue and red across their faces and necks and sporting leather saddles on their back, folded their spindly legs and descended on their haunches in robotic fashion to take on the excited tourists. As they rose back to their lofty heights, the smiles on the faces of the adventure seekers seemed to wane while they clung to the hump of the camel for added stability. The camel commenced galloping at a reasonable pace with its trainer following on foot. Grimacing cronies with their cameras had a heyday selling their mug shots at fleecing prices to gullible buyers. My husband and I were very content watching the show from our relatively secure sand-covered benches.

Back in Tangier at sunset, we headed to an eatery for "Berber Pizza"—round bread stuffed with spices, almonds and vegetables. For dessert we sampled the popular Morvenpick ice cream "Vanilla Dream," made with Bourbon Vanilla for a distinct flavor.

We boarded the ferry next morning for a "hop" across the Straits of Gibraltar to Andalusia's most beautiful city Seville for a two-night stay.

From the boat, we had a glimpse of the Rock of Gibraltar, a mountainous elevation protruding into the sea at the southern tip of Spain. Our guide briefly filled us in on a few interesting details as we cruised along. The massive brick building on the rock with a fluttering Union Jack was originally a Moorish castle but stands today on British territory as the Tower of Homage. The higher areas on the rock were frequented by migratory birds, partridges and a rare species of apes called "Macaques." As we neared the Spanish coast, we could not but wave a teary goodbye to Morocco – a land that gave us the Arabian Night feel in all its splendor and one of the few countries which afforded its tourists a panorama of snow capped glaciers existing within driving distance from the seemingly infinite sand stretches of the Saharan desert.

Back to the port town of Algeciras in Spain, we resumed our motor coach ride to Seville driving past the Jerez vineyards, which are home to Andalusia's finest sherry. Seville, we were told, embodied the heart and soul of Andalusia—a city brimming to this day with Moorish

influence amidst guitars and whirling skirts of the flamenco dancers. Orange trees, flower filled patios, horse
drawn carriages and time honored architecture served as
ushers to our elegant accommodation in the heart of the
city. This huge three-storied mansion, believed to be commissioned by the King of Spain in 1928 as one of the region's better hotels, displayed Moorish grandeur in its
stately arches, ornamental lighting and classic décor. The
rooms reflected high-end tastes in Spanish elegance.
Frescoes of angels adorned the ceiling, old fashioned elevators with carved doors operated on manual mode, and
the entire structure stood around a courtyard with a fountain, as in all Moorish palaces. The sprawling gardens
were idyllic and intimate—bright orange trees lined the
walkways bringing in a touch of the Mediterranean while
pools, tennis courts, and onsite restaurants had their fair
share of patronizing guests. Victorian horse carriages
drawn by well-fed studs in shiny coats trotted the thoroughfares oblivious of the vehicular traffic whizzing past
them. Some of the foreigners who took the "joy rides" later
told us that it was one of the most romantic experiences of
their life—how and why I could never figure out nor could
I probe further due to the sensitive nature of the topic.

We were warned of petty crimes in the area, especially of brazen bag snatchers. By way of abundant cau-
tion coupled with the onset of dusk, we decided to remain
on the hotel grounds that evening. A typical Andalusian
dinner was served that night in the banquet hall, and
without much ado the fun-loving Spaniards lived it up
with drinks, merry-making and socializing. For starters,
we had fresh baked country bread with an oil and vinegar
dip, and assortments of cold cuts and cheese. The music
and the tempo on the dance floor brought back memories

of the Greek dancers on our Mediterranean cruise, except that ceramic plates were not dashed to the ground here.

The spread was laid out buffet style—there were pigeon and seafood entrées, the vegetarian entrée "huevos a la flamenco" was a delicious egg dish baked with peas, asparagus and peppers, the spicy gazpacho, salads with manzanilla olives, tomatoes, cucumbers and peppers and a lip smacking dish of potatoes in garlic sauce which the Spanish call "ajoharina." Stuffed to the hilt with the many delicacies, we did not venture in the direction of the dessert table. We wrapped up the evening with Rioja wine and cold Sangria before retiring for the night.

Next morning, we were slated to see the Giralda Tower, the Maria Luisa Park and the famous cathedral of Seville. The all Spanish local tour guide came across as having been on the job for many years. He was personable, knowledgeable, and savvy. He came around warmly shaking hands with each of us on the motor coach before embarking on his running commentaries. "Señores and señoras, you are a very fortunate group of people, not only because you have had an opportunity to visit this historic Andalusian city, but also because you have been put up in the hotel which was home to Peter O'Toole and Omar Sharif when they were here shooting scenes for *Lawrence of Arabia*." He chuckled to himself as he watched elation written large on our faces! I wanted him to go on, but our first stop had already arrived.

The Giralda Tower, looming over 300 feet high, was built in the late 1180s on the ruins of a Moorish mosque of bygone eras and currently served as the Bell Tower of the Cathedral of Seville. Though it presented an architectural mix of the Almohad, Gothic and Roman styles, its sheer immensity still remained an inspiration in spite of the face changes it went through with each regime that came to power. Negotiating the sloping ramps to ascend the tower wasn't exactly a breeze, but once up there it was a rewarding climb indeed. The adventurous few continued on to the bell tower at the top while the rest of us settled for the landing two-thirds way up, which gave us a dramatic view of the city. Perched on this magnificent minaret, we saw the Guadalquiver River flowing across the city, the cobbled streets in the old quarters, stretches of white-washed villas and the azure waters of the distant ocean. I noticed that the tower sported a large bronze weather vane at the topmost level with the figure of a woman in the center. I was curious as to how and why it belonged there. The guide explained that the tower got its name "Giralda" from the revolving motion of the vane (gira means turning) and the figure of the woman represented the patroness of Faith to the devout Sevillos.

We worked our way down from the tower to enter the famed Cathedral through the Courtyard of Oranges—Patio de los Naranjos as it is popularly known. From this huge serene courtyard fringed with orange and palm trees, we gazed in admiration at the largest medieval Gothic structure in the world and the most venerated place of worship in all of Spain. Formerly an Almohad mosque, it was converted to a cathedral in 1248 by King Ferdinand. The interior of the cathedral was a superior display of Seville's affluence at the time. The thematic décor was in gleaming gold. The central nave and its aisles shone with the precious metal. The "coro" or choir—a huge boxlike structure in the center of the cathedral—opened into the Gothic altar, considered to be the most ornate and largest in the Christian world. There were numerous carved scenes from the life and death of Christ, each meticulously detailed in wood and gold while the 12th century bronze doors still carried inscriptions from the Koran. The sun's rays glinted on the colorful stained glass windows highlighting the art of the artisan. It was hard to tell which of the manmade marvels we had seen transcended into the realms of divine beauty—the Duomo in Milan or the Mosque of Hassan II in Casablanca or the Gothic Cathedral in Seville. We proceeded to the Sacrista Mayor, the designated treasury that housed precious artifacts and artworks. The most fascinating display that caught my attention was the "Keys of Seville" presented to King Ferdinand by the Moorish community at the time of surrender. Sculpted on them in Arabic was an inscription that read "May Allah render eternal the dominion of Islam in this city."

After a brief viewing of the silver shrine that housed the coffin of Fernando III in the Royal Chapel, we headed to the Christopher Columbus Mausoleum. We learned that Columbus died in 1506, an utterly disillusioned man, and that it remains uncertain where he was interred. But according to popular belief, his sepulcher rests here showing pallbearers from the regions of Castilla, Leon, Navarra and Aragon carrying his coffin. On his tombstone were inscribed the prophetic words "a castilla y a leon, mundo nuevo dio colon" (To Castile and Leon, Columbus gave a new world).

After a very satisfying day of sight-seeing we returned to the hotel for an afternoon's siesta with plans to reconvene for the "piece de resistance" of the evening—flamenco dance and dinner at a popular "tabalao" (show venue). Excited as we were at the prospect, I personally was a trifle apprehensive after my recent brush with belly dancing in Morocco. I saw to it that I was conservatively dressed in a Western outfit this time around, and that we seated ourselves at the far end of the restau-

191

rant—inconspicuous and snug in a low-lighted corner. Our tour guide had oriented us on this passionate national dance of Spain so that we could better relate to the hand and footwork during the show. A product of Spanish, Arabic and gypsy cultures, this dance form was believed to have derived its name "flamenco" from the Arabic terminology "felag mengu" meaning fugitive peasant. There have never been formatted guidelines to this type of dance since most performers learned by watching others and some improved on their performance with Spanish ballet classes. We were given the option of meeting the performers backstage before the start of the two-hour show but I discreetly chose to pass up on anything that was likely to bring me in close proximity to the artistes.

The show started with an introduction of the performers: the guitarists, the singers and the dancers—most of whom were beautiful Spanish women in long outfits that were fitted waist up and free flowing in frilled layers waist down. As the guitarist strummed to the tune of Andalusian folk songs, the dancers clapped, stomped their feet, and swished their skirts in keeping with the rhythm of the music. The tempo rose to a crescendo with all the artistes in harmonious unison. The knowledgeable audience rose to give them a big hand at the high point performance. To the uninitiated like me, the dance seemed to be an extempore show of free rhythm, body language, clapping and whirling to the tune of the guitarist and an invitation for the audience to participate. The evening ended with a traditional Andalusian dinner served by folks whose allure for fun and food never fades.

Slated events for the next morning were a half day at Maria Luisa Park, believed to be a veritable fairyland on earth, and a free evening for souvenir hunters. The Maria Luisa Park was undoubtedly one of the loveliest in all of Europe. The picturesque gardens and the marble grounds were home to congregations of innumerable white pigeons that chose to hop dangerously close to us as we strolled along the walkways. The neatly trimmed hedges alongside flowerbeds, fragrant bowers and century-old elms and pines made it a favorite haunt for lovers. We moved on for views of the Fountain of Lions built in Renaissance and Andalusian styles, the Pond of the Lotuses and finally the Islet of the Ducks. It had a central island in the middle of a lake housing a pink and white gazebo looking pavilion with an all-ceramic fountain spouting out a misty drizzle. Sleek-necked swans glided along gracefully, stopping often for cleansing dips in the water. We could have spent all day enjoying the captivating beauty, but our tour guide had a schedule to keep. We were nudged to proceed to the alabaster statue of Poet Gustavo Adolfo Becquer situated under a bare cypress tree. This was probably designed to be the last stop of the day with good reason so that the dreamers amongst us could be jolted back to the din and bustle of the real world.

After a sumptuous breakfast next day, we were on the road again for a five-hour commute to Lisbon. Driving through the barren plateaus of Extremadura, we crossed the border into Portugal at Alentejo, the granary city of the country. Golden wheat fields covered the vast rolling plains, livestock grazed in large countryside farms and cork and eucalyptus forests loomed over stretches of vineyards and olive groves. Patches of townships on the hilltops seemed to play games with our visual acuity—here this minute and gone the next. Crossing the port town of Setubal twenty-five miles south of Lisbon, we were well on our way to Portugal's historic capital that overlooked the Tagus River. Lisbon was a picturesque hilly city with numerous medieval castles, monasteries, and palatial villas, behind the iron gates of which sat vigilant muscular pit bulls. They sprang into "attack" mode even if a vehicle or pedestrian inadvertently slowed down in their vicinity!

We were accommodated in a beautiful "pousada" on the outskirts of Lisbon, the likes of which I had never seen before. Pousadas function out of restored castles, monasteries and fortresses throughout Portugal. Ours was a sprawling convent of the Santiago order situated on the peak of a range of rolling hills overlooking miles of lush vineyards and vegetation. The peace and dignity of an erstwhile nunnery coupled with upscale service and modern comforts made it a popular choice of tourists. The cloistered section of the convent was set apart for reading or meditation, the parlors with their distinguished but restricted décor served as lounges for the guests and the "refectory" of the nuns with stark stucco walls and bare timber ceilings was invitingly arranged to function as a dining hall. As we walked down the spartan hallways under wide arches and horizontal roofs, (I use the word "Spartan" here because all through this trip we were pampered with ornate architecture around us), I was mentally transported to my convent days in a boarding school where our rooms lined such Gothic corridors and we could hear the jingle of the nuns' rosaries and the soft "Hail Marys" as they walked by. The pousada tradition required the staff to know each and every guest by name and go the extra mile to make us feel like houseguests rather than tourists. Dinner that night consisted of Madeira wine and cider, salads, meat entrées, fish cakes, and a vegetarian soup slow cooked with Tuscan bread, vegetables, beans and olive oil. It was more filling than a meal. Custard tarts were served for dessert.

Our sight-seeing next morning commenced with a detailed tour of the magnificent Hieronymite Monastery (a UNESCO world heritage site) which in the late 1400s served as the venerated site for Vasco da Gama and his crew to congregate for divine guidance on the eve of their voyage to India. King Manuel I was believed to have sponsored this extravaganza in stone and it apparently took over a century to reach its present stature. The vast spacious structure was predominantly Manueline in style which, we were told, essentially meant a progression of the Gothic style to Renaissance embodying some Spanish Renaissance as well in the form of "Plateresco" engraving in silver workmanship. The double-storied ornamental entry to the monastery looked like a shrine in its own right. The Manueline architecture came alive in the stone work carved with nautical motifs and signature emblems of royalty.

We followed the throng of visitors to enter the building through the Southern Portal amidst gables and pinnacles. In the center stood the statue of Prince Henry the Navigator, around which were carved niches with scenes from the life of the Patron Saint Jerome. The serene atmosphere was further accentuated by the image of Virgin Mary on a pedestal atop the moldings and above it was a statue of Archangel Michael. Traversing through the Western Portal into the church of Saint Maria, the lavish ornamentation of the interior and the emphasis on carved columns, arches and niches unequivocally pronounced the Renaissance style. At the ingress were the patriotic shrines of Vasco da Gama—Portugal's worshipped voyager—and Luis de Camoes, the country's celebrated poet.

195

Vasco da Gama was believed to have been buried in Saint Francis church in Cochin, India in 1524 before his remains were moved to this hallowed spot in Lisbon. A prostrate figure of Vasco da Gama carved in marble lay on top of the sarcophagus. Its sides were engraved in Manuelina relief with the emblem of a sailing ship surrounded by carvings of leafs and flowers. The entire structure rested on six crouched lions detailed in stone.

Having journeyed through the splendor of Portugal's heritage, we proceeded to the "Monument of Discovery"—a comparatively recent memorial honoring Prince Henry the Navigator. Towering to 170 feet it looked like the "prow" of a sailing ship with figures of famous voyagers, nationals and kings congregated on the starboard side.

The Belem Tower on the waters of the Tagus River was our last stop for the day. Built in 1515 to protect the harbor, it has stayed on as a symbolic remembrance of Portugal's voyages that helped usher wealth into the country. Even over the centuries, it still has retained its stature in Moorish style watchtowers, trellised corridors, arcaded windows and most importantly a statue of Our Lady of Safe Homecoming for the homeward bound Portuguese sailors.

The rest of the day was ours to explore on our own. After a much needed afternoon "siesta," my husband and I decided to spend the evening in Bairro Alto an old section of town, listening to the haunting "Fado" melodies, and later trying a traditional Portuguese dinner. Since we were totally alien to the world of Fado, I had expected an evening of lilting and jazzy music by candlelight. On the contrary, we found ourselves in a dimly lit café listening to a sad and soulful rendering in Portuguese by a singer who seemed steeped in even more melancholy. The accompanying guitarist didn't help any to relieve the mood of pain and anguish. So, this was the world of traditional Fado! We could not endure it for too long and quickly exited through a side door hoping that the Portuguese dinner would be our mood lifter for the evening. And it sure was. After Madeira wine for an aperitif, we were pleasantly surprised at the choice of available vegetarian dishes though they came with a price tag of difficult translation. I personally could wander away from the political correctness of vegetarianism, but not my husband. The yellow split pea soup with toasted garlic was delicious followed by a colorful plate of salad. The vegetable entrée Tamale Pie—a black bean stew topped with cheddar and a layer of fresh corn bread—was lip-smacking good. "Café com Leite" (similar to American latte) and Passion fruit Mousse concluded the dinner.

A scenic two-hour drive next morning through the Serra d'Aire Mountains brought us to the world's most celebrated scene of religious miracles—The Shrine at Fatima. This was where Virgin Mary had appeared to three peasant children in 1917, one of whom was an aging Carmelite nun in Coimbra, Portugal. The imposing basilica built in neo-classical style stood on the far end of the huge square. At the spot where the apparition was sighted, stood the Cova housing the Chapel of Apparitions. The unending stream of the faithful trekking towards the shrine could be seen from miles away. The disabled, the maimed, the ever grateful and the devout stood patiently in line across the basilica square to light candles or offer a "Novena" or simply pray to Our Lady of Fatima at the church altar. Some crawled on their knees for over 100 feet down a slope to the chapel, in fulfillment of their vows. After lighting candles near the little chapel where Virgin Mary had appeared, we walked to the main basilica—Sanctuary of Fatima. Above the entrance way to the cathedral was a white marble statue carved in a niche showing Virgin Mary as she appeared in one of her apparitions. The painting above the high altar depicted the message of "Our Lady" to the little peasant children. Stained glass windows carried scenes of the sightings. Our Lady of Fatima was believed to have made three appearances to the shepherd children in a pasture and the last of the sighting happened in torrential rains when crowds had gathered to witness the Solar Miracle of Fatima. The story goes that for a few brief moments the sun changed colors, spun in the sky and momentarily seemed to plunge towards earth. Although born into the Hindu faith, we personally felt an immense sense of peace and serenity as we knelt in prayer in the pews of the church. An inexplicable grace seemed to pervade our very being and as we stepped out of the cathedral we found ourselves headed towards the church souvenir store although we had no directions to get there nor did we intend buying anything. We ended up buying a three-dimensional framed portrait of Our Lady of Fatima which we kept in the worship area of our home. Since then, many unlikely blessed events have occurred in our family.

From the Fatima Shrine we walked up a two-mile cobblestone pathway past the fourteen Hungarian Stations of the Cross to a marble chapel of Christ. It is believed that the peasant children took this path to Cova da Iria to await the apparition of Virgin Mary. After a brief lunch of soup and sandwiches we were back on the coach crossing the border back into Spain, en route to Salamanca. We were in for a fairly long haul and reached there in time to take in the astounding ambience of the most beautiful plaza in the country. The four-storied structure around the paved open air seating was Baroque inspired with symmetrical arches at the ground level serving as entrances into the plaza. Boutiques and trinket shops, cafes and restaurants, and unsolicited musical groups performing in the square, kept the place bustling with activity.

We checked in for the night's stay at a hotel, which again was a restored castle in the heart of the historic district. In the final phase of the tour heading back to Madrid, we stopped at the walled town of Avila, which was the birthplace of Saint Teresa, the Patron Saint of Spain. The convent of Saint Teresa was built in the 17th century on the spot where her house once stood. She has been hallowed worldwide for performing miracles. The story goes that when she died in her monastic cell in 1582, a heavenly fragrance permeated the area. 330 years later when her body was exhumed, her coffin emitted the exact same fragrance. At the Sala De Reliquias of the convent church, we saw exhibits of her relics—the piece of wood she used as a pillow, a finger from her right hand, her rosary beads and the cord that she used to lash herself as an act of penance.

We reached Madrid in time to check into our hotel, bid our trip mates "adios" and prepare for our flight back to the United States the next day, concluding the visit to a region where history has endured through the cultures of its people and preservation of its ancient monuments.

This ends the section on travelogue and I crave the indulgence of my readers if I have weighed on their patience with in-depth details of events and scenarios.

Part III

Reflections

The viewpoints expressed herein are solely the author's opinions.

Fifteen
The New Millennium—2001

The year 2001 was one of the darkest periods in American history—the year when the horrific 9/11 tragedy occurred as the world watched in shock and dismay. It was as though a Tsunami of hatred and revenge had swept through the country leaving in its wake unimaginable death and destruction.

September 11 that year was a bright sunny day in Upstate New York. I had turned on the television a little past 8:30 A.M. as was my daily practice. Nothing seemed ominous or different that fateful morning. I had hardly settled into the sofa with my cup of coffee when I saw the silhouette of an aircraft appear in the horizon, headed towards the skylines of New York City. Nothing seemed odd about that either. In a matter of minutes, I watched it plunge into the Twin Towers of the World Trade Center in New York. A terrible plane crash, I thought. Clouds of billowing smoke rose from the North Tower and giant flames leapt through the smoldering structure. A sea of humanity was seen fleeing away from the scene while valiant first responders—the fire trucks, emergency police vehicles, volunteers and rescue teams—sped towards the emblazoned area. People were jumping to their deaths from the burning tower, while some scrambled through the flame-engulfed windows trying to escape into the streets. Debris of ash and body parts rained onto the pavements and parked cars. While rescuers set up command centers at the site, the grim process of recovering charred remains from the mangled tower continued. Television viewers watched in stunned silence as all of the chaos, pandemonium and disarray were being aired.

At this point a second aircraft showed up in the skies and negotiating a slight turn, flew right into the South Tower, torching up another inferno adjacent to the already blazing North Tower. Survivors fled in utter disbelief, unable to figure out what had hit them. Family members frantically tried to access hotline numbers for news of their loved ones. It did not take long for the country to realize that these were no accidental plane crashes—they were cold, calculated attacks on an unsuspecting nation. "Breaking news" on all channels carried the shocking headlines "America under Attack." As details emerged, TV stations broke them live round the clock. Those instantly killed were the passengers on the aircrafts and occupants on the upper floors of the Twin Towers that took the direct hits. International reaction strongly denounced these dastardly attacks that were carried out in the name of "Jihad" (Holy War). Al Qaeda suicide squads were behind these hijackings, believed to be masterminded by Osama Bin Laden.

On that fateful morning of September 11, nineteen terrorists set out on a ruthless mission that claimed thousands of innocent civilian lives and billions of American dollars. Posing as innocuous passengers, they accessed and hijacked four commercial passenger jetliners en route to California from Boston, New York and Washington, D.C. airports. United Airlines Flight 175 was the first to crash into the North Tower a little before 9:00 A.M., followed shortly by American Airlines Flight 11 into the South Tower. A third aircraft, American Airlines Flight

77, flew into the U.S. Department of Defense at the Pentagon in Virginia around 9:30 A.M. killing all aboard and a hundred people on the ground. The fourth airliner, United Airlines Flight 93, was headed in the direction of the White House, crashing into a field in the town of Shanksville, Pennsylvania at 10:00 A.M. but not before a concerted attempt by the heroic crew and passengers to regain control of the aircraft.

Over 3,000 people perished in this orchestrated carnage. Bread winners and loved ones were cruelly snatched away without a final goodbye. Surviving families and victims continue to live in their own world of devastation, while gaping holes remain where Twin Towers once stood. Islam has always been known to be a religion of peace and brotherly love. I remember my childhood years when we lived in harmony as friends and neighbors. Some of my father's trusted colleagues and advisors were Moslems. During Hindu and Moslem high holidays, delicious dishes and mouth-watering sweets were exchanged. On sobering occasions, each rallied around the other in their grief. Today with the advent of fundamentalism, the true tenets of Islam are being hijacked. Their Holy Scriptures have always carried the undisputed word of God, teaching believers how to lead a good life and seek spiritual purity. Today's radical factions are out to achieve one universal Islamic world at the cost of eradicating all other faiths. That is a far cry from the peaceful advocacies of the religion. In the secular Islam summit at St. Petersburg, Florida on March 4, 2007, luminaries and thinkers in the Faith had spoken up for a change—a change that needed to stem from within Islam to weed out terrorism and let humanity practice their individual faiths without fear.

Anticipation of possible terrorist attacks has now resulted in security screenings in all government establishments, airports, and sports arenas to name a few. Body searches, shoe searches, background info scrutiny and detailed questioning if, God forbid, one's name happens to be similar to someone on the "wanted list" (a two-year-old infant was no exception at an airport) have resulted in clamping down the guaranteed freedom of a citizen. I recall the times when we came into this country over three decades ago. We did not come as expatriates or political refugees. We came as legal immigrants to this great land in pursuit of the "American Dream." The U.S. Declaration of Independence in 1776 had mandated "That all men are created equal, that they are endowed by their Creator with certain unalienable rights, that among these are Life, Liberty and pursuit of Happiness." Based on the above premise, the term "American Dream" became especially significant when James Truslow Adams in 1931 defined it in his book *The Epic of America* as "That dream of a land in which life should be better and richer and fuller for everyone, with opportunity for each according to ability and achievement."

America has been a land nurtured by immigrants, be they white, black or brown. It was a nation that had at one time engulfed an entire race in slavery, but yet again fought a Civil War to outlaw segregation and discrimination. It is in these bloodbaths that the real United States was born. Immigrants who traveled here from all corners of the world came for a prosperous life, better opportunities and freedom from persecution. "The cream of intelligentsia" congregated here and made their contributions in different disciplines, resulting in America being the most powerful democratic republic in the world today. History has never been and will never be molded in silence, if democracy needs to move on. The famous Irish statesman Edmund Burke had said "All that is necessary for the triumph of evil is for good men to do nothing." It is in the national interest of Americans to set aside party affiliations and rise as one man to fight aggressions that might have the potential to hurt this great land.

There are a few grave concerns which in my opinion call for a closer look at our personal responsibilities and the governing laws of the land:

Moral Values

Our Founding Fathers had established a secular nation with freedom and liberty for all. But under the banner of secularism, religion in its totality seems to be disappearing from the lives of the younger generation, allowing for a dip in moral values and a rise in promiscuity. I cannot help but mention here a popular quote of President Theodore Roosevelt: "To educate a person in mind and not in morals is to educate a menace to society." These days we hear of increasing teenage pregnancies, fifth graders indulging in classroom sex, teens insanely killing for thrill or vengeance, kids high on drugs and unsupervised teenagers going on horrific shooting rampages in schools, university campuses, malls and churches. Much as we would like to attribute the killings to deranged minds and twisted thought processes, the fact remains that they do stem from a personal sense of low self-esteem. The transition from childhood to adulthood is like an hourglass where time slips away like the grains of sand. I hold career parents in great esteem—individuals who have to juggle their time between work and raising a family. But somewhere along this juggling process, the

‟proper upbringing of children tends to falls through the cracks. The children of today will be the future of tomorrow, the cornerstones and pillars of this prosperous nation and towards that end disciplinary guidance and parental love should form the fabric of child raising. During the children's formative years, rapports with their teachers are also of profound significance. I would like to share with my readers an inspiring poem on the joint role of a teacher and a parent:

Unity

I dreamed I stood in a studio,
And watched two sculptors, there,
The clay they used was a young child's mind,
And they fashioned it with care.

One was a teacher: the tools he used
Were books and music and art,
One a parent with a guiding hand,
And a gentle loving heart.

Day after day the teacher toiled,
With touch that was deft and sure,
While the parent labored by his side,
And polished and smoothed it over.

And then at last their task was done,
They were proud of what they had wrought,
For the things they had molded into the child,
Could neither be sold or bought.

And each agreed he would have failed,
If he had worked alone,
For behind the parent stood the school,
And behind the teacher, the home.

—Anonymous

The Need for Tough Gun Laws in America

The existing gun control and firearm laws in America leave a lot to be desired. Tougher access to automatic weapons and handguns along with stricter licensing regulations would mean condemning less innocents to death. The lax standards of gun ownership in the U.S. and the ease with which guns can be procured defy all logic and reason. Mass tragedies have occurred in recent times triggering tears and fears, indelible pain and haunting memories, all because of a delusional notion that our right to bear arms is a genetic imprint of the American culture.

The Columbine High School tragedy occurred on April 20th, 1999 in Colorado when two students of the school went on a deadly shooting rampage inside the school premises, killing twelve fellow students and a teacher before ending their own lives. One can never surmise what goes on in the twisted dark minds of cold-blooded killers, but the end results undoubtedly are the same—senseless loss of innocent lives.

The Amish schoolhouse massacre on October 2nd, 2002 in Pennsylvania left five young girls dead when a lone thirty-two-year-old gunman shot them execution style mid-morning in the one room school, before killing himself. The Amish community responded with forgiveness as was expected in their culture. But innocent little lives were snuffed away long before their prime because a deranged mind had easy access to a firearm.

The Virginia Tech massacre on April 16th, 2007 was a disaster of monumental proportions that occurred on campus killing thirty-three and injuring twenty-three, making it the deadliest school shooting so far in U.S. history. Within a span of two hours, the mentally ill student turned gunman had randomly mowed down five faculty members and twenty-seven of his peers with semi-automatic handguns within the confines of classrooms on campus before turning the gun on himself. In his own bleak world, this sociopath had had the ultimate last word, leaving in its wake unprecedented horror and human slaughter. Global criticism of U.S. gun laws and gun violence sparked by this needless tragedy led to the passage of a significant federal gun control requiring a criminal background check and halting sale of firearms to the mentally ill and criminals. The U.S. House of Representatives and the Senate passed the legislation in December 2007. The efficacy of this measure however yet remains to be seen. Editorial responses in leading international newspapers remain uniformly doubtful of any viable change in "America's deep rooted and sometimes lethal commitment to its own freedom." (Ref: Media coverage of Virginia Tech massacre on Internet.)

Shooting rampages have now infiltrated into churches and missionary training centers as evidenced in Colorado in the latter half of 2007. Not a day passes without the media reporting violent crime. Regardless of the mental state of these perpetrators, the fact remains that indiscriminate access to guns will only continue to facilitate violence across America. In a statistical evaluation of Civil Arsenals across the globe, United States of America tops the list with 90 firearms/100 persons and with Germany at an all time low of thirty firearms/100 persons. Yemen, Finland, Switzerland, Iraq, France, Canada and Sweden fall in between. Since Americans obviously own more guns than others in the world it is not surprising that we have led the industrialized nations with a firearm death rate of 30,000 in 2007.

We as a nation are obsessed with statistics, facts and figures. And to date we have an unmatched record of crime and violence. America's laws go all out to defend people's rights and to uphold freedom of speech and freedom to bear arms. But what about upholding the basic right of an individual to live? Are we as a nation getting desensitized to human carnage? Guns are deadly assault weapons and now they apparently come in pink, red, green and blue colors. Is this an attempt to make them more attractive to a deranged mind or will accessorizing them in this fashion make the pain and suffering of the unsuspecting victims more acceptable? The Second Amendment to the Constitution was formulated in the 1780s promulgating the settlers' rights to bear arms in self-defense or while serving in a state militia. There were genuine concerns at the time of attacks from bandits, pirates, and local natives as well as the possibility of a tyrant rising to leadership. But in this day and age every state in the U.S. has its own National Guard and law enforcement to ensure its security. America has the most powerful military arsenal in the world today and an individual's right to own a firearm is redundant and possibly contributing to the escalating rate of violence in this country. Most of the carnages have been perpetrated by disturbed and violent minds gaining power through easy access to assault weapons.

A sample of combating gun crimes in advanced nations show an "across-the-board" temperance in gun laws.

Handguns are banned in Great Britain to the point that even participants of their Olympic teams have to practice outside British soil. In Sweden, civilians have to have a crime-free record and possess a hunting license before acquiring firearms. Italy requires a valid reason for possessing a gun. In China, private citizens have no recourse to firearms. Japan prohibits handguns while strictly regulating firearm permits. Australia's tough gun control laws prohibit automatic assault weapons while strict licensing restrictions further ensure the safety of their citizens. Russia outlaws handguns and a license for hunting rifles calls for several documents including a mental health clearance. Brazil's gun laws validate gun permits only to law enforcement personnel and others serving in high-risk professions. France requires sanction of a hunting permit before granting ownership of firearms.

Gun enthusiasts in the United States might contend that the victims of gun tragedies were in the wrong place at the wrong time. But such philosophy does nothing for the distraught, grieving families of the hapless victims who were mercilessly mowed down by sadistic murderers. It is certainly time for our lawmakers to take a good, hard look at the existing gun laws in the U.S. before it seriously begins to taint the "American Dream." At the very least, a commonsense gun control legislation should be put in place.

The Criminal Justice System

Media reports of violent murderers, rapists, abductors and pedophiles allowed back on the streets of America due to laxity in the enforcement of the law or loopholes in the system or overcrowding in prisons, forebodes a possible breakdown of the criminal justice system in the years to come. Thanks to aggressive lobbying by the grieving families of raped and murdered children, we now have made some headway in the form of Megan's Law passed by the U.S. Congress in 1996 and Jessica's Law introduced in Florida in February 2005. Seven-year-old Megan Kanka was kidnapped, raped and murdered by a violent pedophile that lived across the street from her home. Megan's Law now mandates notifying the public when a convicted sex offender moves into the neighborhood. Jessica Lunsford was a nine-year-old Florida girl who was abducted under cover of darkness, raped in captivity for a few days and finally buried alive by the convicted sex offender. The key provisions of this law call for a mandatory minimum prison sentence of twenty-five years and a lifetime of electronic monitoring of the pedophile. Forty-two states in the U.S. have since introduced the legislation, which bolsters harsher measures in dealing with these peccant criminals.

The "Amber Alert" put out by law enforcement personnel and broadcasting stations also helps to some extent in alerting the public of a possibly abducted or missing child in jeopardy. But all the same cold, calculated and heinous crimes continue to plague the nation while defense attorneys of the perpetrators file endless appeals highlighting temporary insanity or retardation.

It is a common occurrence for activists against the death penalty to congregate outside the gates of the prison grounds for a candlelight vigil on the eve of an execution. But does it not tug at people's heart strings to imagine the plight of the innocent victims whose lives have been brutally cut short in their prime—pregnant young women clobbered or strangled to death, unsuspecting victims of botched robberies raped and murdered in cold blood, hikers in pursuit of their passion strangled on forest trails, a little girl fast asleep on her bed surrounded by her stuffed animals abducted in the thick of night, repeatedly raped and finally lured into a plastic bag for a live burial while she poked her fingers through the bag for a breath of air in her final agonizing moments? There were no makeshift memorials to mark the shallow graves of these doomed victims nor were there any candlelight vigils to mourn their fate. Most recently in June '08 the Supreme Court ruled 5–4 a blanket prohibition on the death penalty for child rape conviction in the state of Louisiana on the grounds that it was not a "proportional punishment" for the crime. Shocking as the ruling is, it's more than obvious that the justice system does not share the pain and irreversible mental trauma of violated little children and their basic rights to human dignity.

I have served as a juror in the U.S. courts as part of a citizen's civic duty. To me, and I emphasize it is entirely my opinion, it seems as though there is a protective protocol in place for every criminal who then starts to believe that he is indeed the victim of an unfair social system. Of course the premise of the judiciary in this country that an accused is deemed innocent till proven guilty, is also a pertinent backdrop to the scenario. The hardened and condemned criminals deserve to be held accountable for their actions and brought to swift justice upon conviction instead of biding time as a "Guest of the Correctional Facility" at the taxpayers' expense. A chill runs down my spine, as I am sure it does for most, to watch media reports of little babies thrown into microwave ovens or dumped in trash bins in freezing temperatures, of toddlers flung into swirling waters by a birth parent or held down in water laden bathtubs till their tiny, vibrant bodies went limp. And all this probably under an "insanity plea." The cold, hard, unflinching demeanors of the ruthless killers should bounce back at them in the form of the frigid arms of justice. Further, there should be no cut-off age limits for perpetrators of heinous crimes. Young or old, they should face the consequences alike. Only then will punishment serve as a deterrent to crime.

Healthcare Crisis in America and Malpractice Issues

Healthcare in America today is facing an unprecedented crisis and unless addressed emergently, we might well be up against a brick wall in the near future. There is a constellation of issues compounding this impasse. Nearly forty-seven million Americans including 9 million children are uninsured due to the increasingly prohibitive costs of healthcare in the U.S. There are millions more that are under insured and probably a major illness away from bankruptcy. Affordable healthcare is a fundamental and reasonable expectation of every man, woman and child in America. It is not just an agenda that surfaces in the election year calling for eloquent debates among political contenders—it is a very real and basic American issue. Even to the most consistently hardworking, aspiring and conscientious citizen, the "American Dream" will continue to remain a dream if systemic problems within the structure are not addressed.

Medicare reimbursements to physicians are on a downward trend while their office overheads increase annually by at least 5 percent. For 2008, the projection points to a further 10 percent cut in Medicare payments and that might well force physicians to limit or even refuse newer Medicare patients. Malpractice premiums rose by 10 percent to 14 percent each year in the past and projected to go up by 20 percent annually for the next five years. It is not just the neurosurgeons, or the obstetricians or the orthopedic surgeons that are most affected by the spiraling insurance premium rates. MDs in all specialties are feeling the heat. The alarming rising rates in some states are forcing healthcare givers to relocate. Added to this, are the frustrating mandates of insurance companies run by non-physicians that have started to dictate to the physician how to practice medicine! The medicos are professionals with years of training behind them, driven men and women who have opted to serve the cause of the sick and the suffering, and sometimes having to navigate through turbulence and intricacies in their medical careers. The day is not far off when this dedicated group will be forced to think in terms of quitting their opted profession, in utter disgust.

Like most other developed nations, a universal health care system funded at the federal level might be a step in the right direction. It is up to our lawmakers to work on that.

The conceptual system of "malpractice" in America has its definitive advantages in giving the aggrieved patients and their families a fair chance of representation in court. There are told and untold stories of botched surgeries, willful neglect, wrong diagnoses, mistaken identities and other obviously outrageous medical errors which justify patients resorting to litigation. But unfortunately, hopes of multi-million dollar settlements have lately become permanent fixtures in the minds of the "sue-happy" patients who try to use the physician's malpractice coverage as a medium to become instant millionaires.

I shall narrate here the details of an eighteen-million-dollar malpractice lawsuit that I personally watched unfold. It occurred in 1996 in an emergency room in upstate New York. A mother brought in her three-month-old infant to the ER with a complaint of fever and cold. The ER physician on duty duly examined the child and appropriate tests were performed including a complete blood cell count and urine analysis. The child was observed in the ER for a couple of hours for interaction and oral fluid intake. On being found to be normal, smiling, playful, and interacting well, the infant was discharged with an initial diagnosis of upper respiratory infection and possible early ear infection. A script for amoxicillin was given and the mother was instructed to follow through with her own pediatrician or return to the ER if the condition were to worsen.

As ill luck would have it, the infant was back in the ER after nine hours with the complaint that the child was not feeling well. He did look sicker and a repeat blood work this time showed a possible early bacterial infection. An immediate pediatric consult was called and a spinal tap performed on the infant. The test revealed bacterial meningitis. Appropriate antibiotics were intravenously administered and the infant transferred to a tertiary care facility. The illness took a stormy course and the child was permanently disabled with severe neurological deficits.

After a year and a half, the ER physician and the hospital where the child was initially seen, were named as defendants in a whopping eighteen-million-dollar lawsuit that covered extended care, pain and suffering. The hospital settled out of court for $50,000, leaving the ER physician holding the bag for the balance. Undaunted and confident that he had done no wrong and had not in any way deviated from the standard of care, the ER physician decided to let the case go to trial rather than settle out of

217

court for a million dollars. The case prolonged for two years with frequent postponements requested by the plaintiffs. This further served to enhance the continuing mental anguish of the defendant. Eventually in the end of January 2000, it came up for hearing before the judge and a six-member jury.

The prosecution's opening statement unequivocally held the ER physician liable for the outcome and damages. Their expert witness who was a board-certified pediatrician testified that a lumbar puncture (spinal tap) should have been performed on the infant even on the first ER visit, his premise being that the mother's previous offspring died of meningitis. The expert witness for the defense—a renowned author of textbooks in pediatric emergency medicine and chief of pediatric ER in a university hospital—opined in court that the defendant had followed all procedural requirements and had in fact exceeded the expected standard of care. The defendant finally took the stand and contended that if indeed this child that came in smiling, playful, and interacting well, exhibiting no signs of sepsis whatsoever, needed a spinal tap in the very first visit to the ER, then every infant presenting with low-grade fever should be subject to the invasive procedure of lumbar puncture. And that certainly was not the acceptable practice of medicine in the United States of America.

The six-member jury deliberated for over half a day and returned with a unanimous verdict of "not guilty." That was the day of deliverance for the physician and his family. I was privy to the proceedings every step of the way because I happened to be the defendant's wife. Lawsuits such as these tend to make physicians wary of their patients resulting in the practice of defensive medicine, which in turn contributes to the rising health care costs.

Litigations that are filed without adequate merit should face a heavy contingent penalty in the event of the plaintiff losing the case, and hopefully that will cut into the growing trend of frivolous lawsuits.

I recall the time when we arrived in America for a better life and a better future. Over three decades later we still see ourselves as having made the right choices. America is a great country and Americans are a resilient people who can adeptly bounce back from adversities and move on to greater heights. Despite their differences, they nurture a passion for freedom, faith in their entrepreneurial talent and the ability to accept diversity in their array of immigrants. George Bernard Shaw had said, "Some men see things as they are and ask why. Others dream things that never were and ask why not." It is not just where our dreams take us, but also where we choose to take our dreams and be the change we wish to see. Glints of hope and goals of idealism still repose within the soul of this great nation. Belief and faith are integral in compounding hope—a hope that extends beyond borders, boundaries and constraints of time. In the chaotic and controversial era that we currently live in, an acculturate approach embodying tolerance and human understanding will help compact the world to a playing field of peaceful co-existence. We all have our own unique flaws and looking past our differences could help us garner global respect and support beyond might and power. Can America hope to dream again and will the morrow hold for us new beginnings? Only time will tell.

An inspiring verse from "Salutation to the Dawn":

For yesterday is but a dream
Tomorrow is only a vision,
But today well lived makes every yesterday a
dream of happiness
And every tomorrow a vision of hope.
Look well, therefore, to this day!
Such is the salutation to the dawn.

—By the famous Indian Poet and dramatist
Kalidasa 4th–5th Century A.D.